THE NEW ARCHBISHOP SPEAKS

What does the new Archbishop believe about . . .

What the church is for
What it means to be human
How to find faith
How to understand the Bible
Marriage and families
The Holy Spirit
Why we pray
Justice?

This is the book in which Dr Carey expresses the essence of his thought. Here is the faith that drives him as he takes up the burden of leadership.

The New Archbishop Speaks

George Carey

A LION PAPERBACK
Oxford · Batavia · Sydney

Text copyright © 1991 George Carey
Some material in this book has been previously published in the
following books from Lion Publishing:
    The Lion Handbook of Christian Belief, first published 1982
    Christianity: A World Faith, first published 1985
    The Message of the Bible, first published 1988
    Jesus 2000, first published 1989

Published by
Lion Publishing plc
Sandy Lane West, Oxford, England
ISBN 0 7459 2083 7
Albatross Books Pty Ltd
PO Box 320, Sutherland, NSW 2232, Australia
ISBN 0 7324 0484 3

British Library Cataloguing in Publication Data
    Carey, George
    The new archbishop speaks.
    I. Title
    233
    ISBN 0-7459-2083-7

Printed and bound in Great Britain by Cox & Wyman Ltd,
Reading

Preface

When it was announced in the summer of 1990 that the new Archbishop of Canterbury was to be me, scores of journalists and media pundits had to start digging for information. Who was this George Carey? Mine had not been among the top few names on people's lists, so I was an unknown quantity.

I am grateful to those journalists who have tried to transmit the personality and the life story of the man who in April will begin the task of leading the Church of England.

But it is not who I am that matters most. It is what I believe. The motive force for all my service and leadership is the faith I hold. And I honestly think this is what people really want to know about.

What does this new archbishop believe about God? What does he think the church is really for? How does he understand human nature?

This short book begins to answer such questions. It takes its readers to the heart of what I believe about some central issues of faith and life.

Let me acknowledge immediately that most of the chapters are not freshly written. With all the rush of preparation, I would not have had time to write a new book. But fortunately, Lion Publishing have commissioned numerous chapters from me during the past eight or nine years, as part of three or four major multi-contributor books on Christian themes. So there, ready to hand, was a quarry of writing which could be used to answer the question, What does the new archbishop believe?

I have simply worked through these chapters to make sure they are as I now want them, and added an introduction and an epilogue.

Such a book, then, fulfils a useful and timely function. But plainly it has its limitations. A number of chapters are very short: simply introducing their themes. And although lot of central beliefs are covered, some are missing—inevitably, because of how the book arose. There is a short piece on what Jesus' death means, for example, but nothing on the resurrection. So please, reader, do not go away thinking George Carey doesn't think the resurrection is important. I do; it's fundamental.

Also, although these chapters describe the core of my thinking, they do not represent its leading edge. I was asked, in each case, to give an account for the non-specialist reader of what Christian belief is on certain subjects. The issue of how these beliefs can be applied to our society today is touched on, but obviously much more needs to be said.

Yet I stand by this little book. And it expresses a very important part of me. I am convinced that we will only get our practice right and solve problems, in society and church, if we base that practice on beliefs which are true and deep.

Here are many of the beliefs which drive me as I humbly take up this office. I invite you to inspect them, and perhaps to ask yourselves your own question: Is this what I believe too?

Contents

How My Own Faith Began   9

PART 1 *What Does It Mean to be Human?*

1   What Does It Mean to be Human?   16
2   God the Creator   37
3   A World Gone Wrong   40
4   Marriage and the Family   42
5   Men and Women Together   44
6   Our Attitude to Money   46
7   Justice: God's and Ours   48

PART 2 *What is the Gospel?*

8   Good News of Freedom   52
9   Finding Faith   63
10   God our Father   78
11   A Covenant with God   81
12   God's Laws   84
13   The Holy Spirit   87

14	God in a Human Life	90
15	The Death of Jesus	93
16	The Kingdom of God	96
17	Making People Whole	98

PART 3 *How Do We Live Christian Lives?*

18	Baptism	102
19	How to Pray	105
20	Worshipping God	108
21	What is the Church for?	111
22	Gifts of the Spirit	114
23	God's Servants	117
24	Sent by God	120

PART 4 *How Can We Understand the Bible?*

25	How Can We Understand the Bible?	124
26	The Book of Books	128
27	The Authority of Jesus' Teaching	134
28	How God Has Made Himself Known	140
29	Does the Bible Speak Today?	142

| EPILOGUE | The Decade of Evangelism Begins | 148 |

How My Own Faith Began

I sometimes smile to myself when I contemplate my journey through life. Here am I, the new Archbishop of Canterbury, in a long line of archbishops going back 1,500 years, and yet a person who came from a most unlikely and indeed most humble home. I am often asked: What does it feel like? Surely you must be overawed by the sense of history? Isn't it rather odd that someone from your kind of background should become leader of such a church?

My response to the last question is swift: 'Not a bit of it. To be Archbishop of Canterbury does not mean that you must come from a noble family or from a certain level of society. It is a result of following Jesus and having the relevant gifts and experience for the job ahead.'

But let me tell you my story.

I was born in the East End of London, the eldest of five children. Who knows where our family originated from? We are related to families with names like Gurney, Donoghue and so on—so it is possible that our family came from Ireland. But leaving that aside, my earliest memories are of happiness and poverty. Happiness because mum and dad were in love and remained in love until they parted temporarily from one another in death. I grew up with that precious gift of being loved—in a home full of laughter and enjoyment. With two brothers and two sisters I had a very normal childhood.

But we were also very poor. Dad was an ordinary working-class man, untrained in anything particularly; very good with his hands and skilful at making and repairing things. We certainly never suffered from lack of food—although I gathered later in life, from things my mother said, that she and dad often went without food in order to feed us. She patched our clothes with care and made sure we were clean and tidy.

Then war came. We were bombed out and we went to live in Dagenham in Essex, where I spent most of my childhood and teenage years.

Church was then a building about half a mile away. I had been baptized in the Church of England but I had no idea what it was all about. I can recall that God came a great deal into our conversation at home, but the church rarely if ever. My mother and father believed in God and knew him as a person to be reckoned with, but their faith was hazy. God was a tolerant, kindly person who, rather along the lines of Mr Micawber's philosophy in Dickens' novel, turned up in the nick of time when people needed help!

My brother Bob, four years my junior, started to go to Sunday school at the age of ten with one of his friends. He went regularly and it seemed to make a great difference to his life. At school he got an almighty teasing; 'creeping Jesus' was one of the taunting expressions used of him. But Bob did not appear to mind; he would shrug his shoulders and laugh.

He asked me one day to go to church with him. Why not? I thought. So I went one Sunday evening. My recollections are now very hazy but some memories stay with me. It wasn't the slightest what I expected. I was surprised that the people there were real people. There were people I recognized and—a surprise this—there were actually people of my own age too!

I'm afraid the service did not mean much. People often romanticize the Book of Common Prayer these days.

Well, I can tell you I didn't understand much of it. I was seventeen, intelligent, but I found it mysterious and obscure. I managed to survive the services by imagining monkeys swinging to and fro, up, over and round the screen which separated nave from chancel.

But the vicar was a good preacher and he held my interest. I went along to some youth gatherings and met people of my own age. I was particularly impressed by two twin brothers, David and John, who invited me to their home to listen to music, and many a Saturday I spent listening to classical music in their home.

But gradually another kind of music began to echo in my spirit—the music of faith. I found many of my questions being answered. You have to understand that I have always been a deeply-thinking person. I had been brought up through the insecurity of the war. The world was manifestly an uncertain and cruel place. I needed convincing that there was a God who cared for me. And if he cared for me, was he a God whom I could know? And if so, how?

Gradually, the character of God took shape as I read books about him. Most importantly I read the greatest of all books, the Bible. Until then, the Bible had been a foreign book to me, and initially I had some problem finding my way round it. I started reading John's Gospel, and as I did so the meaning of Christianity seemed to become clearer.

I saw the importance of Jesus for faith. This person, who up to then had been just a mysterious historical figure, began to take shape. His personality began to come through the pages of the Gospel. I was impressed by his teaching, his behaviour and lifestyle. Above all, his death impressed me, and what I read about his resurrection troubled me.

Resurrection? Yes, it seemed to need a question-mark at the time. I could not quite believe that a person could come back from the dead. It seemed to contravene all

11

experience; like many, I resisted the notion. But I read about it and tried to keep an open mind.

One book made me think deeply: *Who Moved the Stone?* by Frank Morrison. The writer produced argument after argument. He showed that all attempts to disprove the resurrection were in fact far weaker than the simple hypothesis that Jesus actually rose from the grave! How could anyone explain the transformation of the disciples, from weak men who ran away at Jesus' time of trial to brave men who were prepared to die for his truth? How could anyone understand the reason for the followers of Jesus, all Jews, changing their holy day from Saturday to Sunday—unless something quite significant happened on that day? There were other arguments that impressed me and led to the dawning conviction that what 'could not happen' actually did!

But the final thing which proved to me that the resurrection actually happened was when I found myself experiencing my own resurrection—a new life seemed to be taking hold of me. Sometime in May 1953 I quietly took a step of faith and committed myself to this God who was in Christ.

There were no flashing lights, angels' voices or trumpets playing the Hallelujah Chorus, just a sense that all was well. My parents had no doubt that I was somehow 'different'. I was clearly under new ownership and with a sense of real joy I could say: 'Yes, now I know I am a Christian!'

From that time my faith in Jesus has not rested simply on rational argument, but also on personal experience. Jesus is someone I know for myself; he is part of my daily life. Nothing less than such a person-to-person meeting can carry us through the ups and downs of our lives.

Looking back I guess four factors were decisive. The local church helped me, encouraged me and challenged me. The Christians there gave me the kind of friendship and support that made the journey possible. My willingness to question was important, too. But once convinced, I was ready to submit to what I found to be true. The Bible made a deep impact on my life; what I read in it changed my way of thinking and living. And then the whole thing was sealed by the presence of God, as he drew closer to me in prayer, worship and study.

This, very simply, was the start of my journey into faith. And that journey still continues. I am more convinced than ever of the truth of the Christian faith, and it is my desire to preach it and live it to the very best of my power.

PART 1

What Does It Mean to be Human?

God made us. He invented humanity. And so human life—your life and mine as well as the life of society as a whole—works best when lived God's way. In this part we consider some aspects of our lives together. But we begin by thinking, What is human nature? Are people basically good or evil? What difference does it make that the world is God's creation?

1

What Does It Mean to be Human?

A school sixth form once agreed in open debate that 'the hope of civilization lies in the pursuit and application of scientific knowledge'. Religion had no place in a utopian society. This life was all, so let us enjoy it. At the end of term, the students asked the headmaster for their job and college references. This was how he phrased one of them:

Biological description John is a living organism. Group: vertebrata. Class: mammalia. Order: primates. Genus: homo. Species: sapiens.

Body structure Organs, tissues, cells—protoplasm. Five organs of sense: sight, taste, touch, sound and smell.

Chemical description A large quantity of carbon. Some gallons of water; various amounts of iron, calcium, magnesium, phosphorus, sulphur, lime, nitrogen, and some mineral salts.

Psychological description A mind, conscious and unconscious; intellectual, emotional and volitional powers; various instincts. IQ 130. 'I hope that John will fit as an admirable unit into the various machines, industrial, commercial and so on, that make up our scientifically-planned society. But regrettably I have serious misgivings about this. There is something in John that refuses to be 'cribbed, cabined and confined' and reaches out to a fulfilment beyond the capacity of a machine-like destiny to supply. In his eager pursuit of scientific knowledge and passionate love of music, as well as in the deep discontent to which he once confessed at his inability to live up to his own ideals, it seems to me that John is on a quest that existence, even in a four-dimensional space-time continuum, can never satisfy.'

Naturally the students had to ask for other more 'real' references. Accurate scientific descriptions were not enough. They left out of their account what it is to be human.

What does the Bible teach about the real nature of humanity?

THE IMAGE OF GOD

In some ways we are no different from any other species on earth. We are creatures subject to the usual conditions of space and time. But we know that human beings 'stand out' from other beings in several ways. Some of these are plain enough; they partly explain humankind's superiority over other creatures: our creativity, our intellectual, linguistic and cultural achievements.

But the Bible adds a further and remarkable point. People stand out not by what they do but by what they are. This is expressed right at the beginning, in the creation story of Genesis 1. God said, 'Let us make man in our image and after our likeness.' It is a theme taken up and developed in other parts of the Bible: we are not like the other creatures; we share God's nature in a special way.

What do we reflect of God?
It is difficult to be very precise about what this sharing of God's nature means, though many theologians have tried.

The main point behind this very important Bible idea of the 'image' is that humanity has been created for a special relationship with God, intended to be personal

17

and eternal. We are above the rest of creation and given 'dominion' over it, not because of the things we can do, but because of the intimate relationship which God wants to share with us. In the Bible 'doing' is always secondary to 'being'. As God intended us, we were called to live life fully in his presence, developing spiritually, mentally and morally as children of God on whom the Creator delights to pour his love.

'Made in God's image' therefore describes us as people who are open to God's call and able to respond to his claims. Yet within this very general picture of humankind's close relationship with God there are particular features which stand out:

True knowledge of God and holiness. We were not created morally neutral. The Bible asserts that we were created as moral beings and that our relationship with him is intended to be one of transparent purity and holiness. The modern assumption is that our moral sense comes through education and group pressure; Christian teaching is that God created us with the knowledge of right and wrong. The coming of sin into human life, however, affected not only our moral state but also, more seriously, our relationship with God.

Intellectual power. We are rational creatures and share in God's rationality which is seen in creation. Humankind's intelligence can be seen in the urge towards creativity—in art, science, religion, play. But, as with every other part of our nature, this creativity has been infected by the blight of sin. None of our achievements has ever come out quite untainted; we have found ways of using all of them for some harmful purpose.

Spirituality. The Bible teaches that we are made for fellowship with God. As the Westminster Confession so beautifully puts it: 'The chief end of man is to glorify God and enjoy him for ever.' We can only find true self-expression and deep fulfilment when we find him.

Immortality. We were made for eternal life with

God. This is the clear teaching of the Bible. It not ours by nature. It is God's gift to his children. Opinions differ about whether humanity was originally created immortal. Some argue that death only came into the world when humankind sinned. Others hold that humanity, according to the Bible, is just as much 'flesh' as the rest of the animal kingdom, and that the 'death' that came with the fall is not physical death, but spiritual separation from God.

Dominion. The Genesis account speaks in the same breath of our creation in the image of God and our dominion over the rest of creation. Our higher position in creation is God-given. He is Lord of all, and in a limited fashion we share in lordship. The whole story sets out in full technicolor the glory and honour with which humanity is crowned and the awesome responsibility that comes with it.

All this makes it plain that the Bible idea that we were created in the image of God is a crucial tool for a Christian understanding of human nature. The vivid story of the idyllic life in Eden gives expression to a real relationship with God which was meant to endure.

Primal tragedy

Humanity has fallen from its destiny and calling. Adam and Eve were confronted with a choice. They chose sin and independence from God. The image of God in humanity has, by that choice, been spoiled and distorted. As the Genesis account portrays it, Adam and Eve were made for fellowship with God and for sharing in his love and generosity. Their fate, through rejection of God, was to be separate from his life. They 'fell' from grace and it became our fall.

As with the account of our creation, so with our fall, there are different views of how to take the story. Some hold that, unless we believe in a literal, historical fall that actually affected the whole human race, we undermine the

19

central Christian facts of sin and salvation. Others see the Genesis story as plainly figurative, describing poetically the deep alienation between God and humanity. The story is saying that we are sinners and need God. Every person is 'Adam' and every person has 'fallen' from the righteousness God intends for us.

The human condition is tragic. Something wonderful has been lost. And yet, even after our fall and in our sin, we have not completely lost the image of God. It is spoilt, but not destroyed.

God's true image

Humanity's fall is not just a theological statement; human history and experience show us that the image has been defaced in us all. As the apostle Paul puts it, 'We have all fallen short of God's standard.' But does this mean that God's image has never been seen in its fullness since the beginning? No, because Jesus Christ is the perfect image of God. That is the New Testament's bold declaration. The task of his mission was to lead us back to God and to restore the image in us.

This is where the New Testament connects the study of Christ with the study of humankind. Because Jesus is both true likeness of God and perfect man, he is the promise of a renewed humanity. To be 'in Christ' is to belong to a 'new humanity', just as to be 'in Adam' is to belong to the old, sinful humanity. The apostle Paul wrote of the 'new nature which is being renewed in knowledge after the image of its creator'. As the 'image of the invisible God', Jesus is the model of what men and women were created to be.

God's grace in the world

Sin is a reality. It is divisive and tragic. But God is still a loving creator. His ultimate purposes are not thwarted by us. Sin and evil never have the last word in God's creation.

God's love is seen as he acts to care for us and to restrain evil. This is expressed in the word 'grace'. Grace is God's way of giving himself freely. We see it in its full glory in Jesus' death on the cross, which shows us just how much God loves us. But God's grace is also experienced in his personal, day-by-day caring and loving. We can distinguish two aspects of grace: 'special' and 'common'.

Special grace refers specifically to God's grace as it reaches those who want to follow Jesus. It is God's way of blessing his people, the church, as he saves them and gives them his Holy Spirit.

Common (or general) grace applies to everyone alive; it stems from God's universal Fatherhood. His grace is received by us all, whether or not we are Christian, as we share in the many blessings of life. Through our sin we have lost any claim on him, yet he still gives abundant tokens of his generosity and goodness day by day. These gifts are showered on all, regardless of creed, character or colour.

Perhaps the clearest expression of God's common grace is as he preserves truth and morality among people. Christians do not have a monopoly of true and good things and neither is morality the province of the Christian alone. Everyone keeps some sense of what is true, good and beautiful, and this is due to God's grace.

Paul sees a further result of this common grace. It opens people's hearts and minds to the goodness of God, and so prepares them to receive God's special grace in Jesus Christ. When we look around at everything good in the world it speaks to us of a loving God who wants us all to know and experience his love and enter into a deeper relationship with him.

HUMAN NATURE

We are 'flesh', made of the 'dust of the earth'. We are part of creation; we eat, excrete, procreate, suffer and die just like the other creatures. The very idea of 'dust' describes our creaturely status. No humanist could speak more definitely of our lowly origins. Far from making us too other-worldly, the Bible cuts us down to size : 'You take away their breath; they die and return to the dust,' says the Psalmist. But if the Bible writers are realistic, they are in no way negative. The Bible affirms life, and joyfully encourages us to enjoy life's pleasures. It tells us that if God has seen fit to create us as physical beings there is nothing in our make-up or anatomy to be ashamed of.

More than animal

But the Bible never stops there. Humankind is mortal, but we are not purely animal. To speak as if we were gives the lie to the idea of the image of God. And so the Bible uses other terms as well: 'soul', 'heart', 'spirit' and 'body'. Taken together with 'flesh', they give us an account of our nature as being open to the worlds both of flesh and of spirit.

The Bible has an integrated view of human nature. It never sees us as the sum total of different compartments: flesh, soul and spirit. The Bible writers were certainly people of their own time and used their own terms to describe humanity. Yet they believed most firmly in what we today call the 'psychosomatic unity' of the person—the interdependence of body, mind and emotions. Body, soul and spirit are terms the Bible uses to show us as people at home in this world, but with the capacity to reach beyond ourselves to the world of the spirit.

The biggest mistake is to think of ourselves as owning a soul as we would a suitcase or an umbrella. This was the way the ancient Greeks thought. Greek or 'Hellenistic' culture was the background to the first centuries of the church. In Alexandria, for instance, theologians tried to relate their faith to this way of thought. Not surprisingly, this Greek view of 'soul' and 'body' infected the early church, whose catch phrase was *soma sema*, 'the body a tomb'. To their mind, the soul was released from its prison at death and set free.

The same idea is expressed in the song: 'John Brown's body lies a-mouldering in the grave, but his soul goes marching on.' It seems to assume that there are two John Browns: the physical John who went to war, now dead, and the spiritual John, now in heaven. It shows how easy it is to fall into thinking that the real 'me' is somehow different from my physical body.

HUMANITY AND NATURE

It is characteristic of people in the West to talk of 'man and creation' as if we were somehow detached from creation. The Bible's teaching questions such an approach. In spite of our special relationship to God, we are still within creation, answerable to the Creator.

Humanity has been set over creation and given 'dominion' over it. We are called to this responsibility of being stewards in God's world. This is true only because we are ourselves creatures and share the same world as other created beings. The history of Western thought has tended to ignore our unity with creation and to exaggerate our independence from it. The education and way of life of modern industrial people tend toward an anti-nature bias, looking on the natural environment as a place to 'use' or 'exploit'.

On the other hand, the tendency in the East (particularly in the religions of the Far East) is to blur the distinction between God, humanity and nature, and this sometimes results in 'Pantheism', the glorification of nature as if it were divine. And even in the West, many television programmes, for instance, speak of 'nature' doing something, as if it were God.

The Bible does not agree with either of these extremes.

It neither confuses God with the world nor separates him from it. Its approach is that God created all things for his pleasure and he delights in the world he has made. He calls into being the bewildering variety of creatures, animate and inanimate, and he wants them all to be fulfilled in their own way. In the modern world we have been forced by the energy-depleted and increasingly polluted earth to think about the ecology of creation and its conservation. The Bible knew about this long ago.

The Old Testament particularly shows striking insight into the connection between a ruined earth and the attitudes of humankind. Isaiah, for example, dwells on the failure of Israel to obey God's laws; he sees the effect not only in social life but in the poisoning of the world around.

We have to face the fact squarely that we are part of nature. Creation is more than our larder, our playground, our sports arena, our theatre of war. It is God's handiwork; we depend on creation more than creation depends on us; it should command our respect.

Our role in nature

'There would be no absolute loss if every human being were to die tomorrow,' said D. H. Lawrence. 'Man is the mistake of creation.' But Lawrence was wrong. The Bible does not view humanity as an accident, nor as an unnecessary appendage to life. We are God's crowning achievement. Without mankind the world would be incomplete and unfinished. In the story of creation, the refrain after each stage is, 'And God saw that it was good.' But not until the climax of the story, the creation of humanity, does the writer say 'God saw everything that he had made and behold it was very good.'

As if to be made in God's image were not privilege enough, humanity's role extends still further. We have been given freedom of choice, and choice implies responsibility. If God calls us to share his nature, it is not surprising that he has given us a distinctive role in the world. We are to be God's agents in the world, representing him and caring for the quality of life: 'Be fruitful and multiply, fill the earth and subdue it and have dominion.' This is not the charter for a despotic tyranny, but it is a summons to be God's co-workers and stewards.

Co-workers

As co-workers with God we are to continue and reflect God's creativity in the world. We do this as we bring to our environment that order, structure and beauty which is our distinctively human contribution. God gains satisfaction and pleasure from his creation; he wants us to take pleasure in it too, as we live in his world and look after it. This shared pleasure opens the door for all kinds of human creativity—in art, music, writing and many other cultural activities.

In the Old Testament, skilled craftsmen were chosen to build the temple—only the best was good enough for God. But some have had a more cramped view of this God-given element. They have overstressed the spiritual side of life and failed to see that one important part of human spirituality is expressed in artistic creativity. Augustine says: 'The beautiful, transmitted through the souls of artists to their hands, comes from that Beauty which is above all souls, for which my soul sighs day and night.'

We cannot but admire Handel's 'Messiah' and Michelangelo's 'The last judgement'. They are great works of art in themselves, as well as expressions of praise and adoration to God. Yet great art does not have to be specifically religious in the wider sense. The creative person, as Keats once said, 'carries out a priest-like task for us', because he opens a window for us through which we see afresh the wonder of life. And wonder puts us in our place; it expresses the gulf between our limited existence and the greatness of creation which dwarfs us.

The Bible, however, does not allow us to glory in our

artistic accomplishments as if they were ends in themselves. Wonder and awe are our response to the creativity of God expressed in nature; human creativity too draws forth its proper response when it moves us to worship God. Humanity is a worshipping species. It is not just that we have a duty to worship our Maker; worship is part of our nature.

We may think that we have a choice between God or nothing. But in fact we all worship something. As Luther said: 'That to which your heart clings is your god.' Our art, our ambition, even our creativity can be the place where our heart rests, and then the true God is replaced. We need a true consciousness of ourselves; we are created beings who live under the eye of a great God, and this must be the cornerstone of all relationships.

The Ten Commandments make this clear. The first commandment, 'You will have no other gods but me', is the basis for all the rest. If we believe that God is our only Lord, respect for his laws and love for others will follow. Jesus summed up this double focus of the law in the twin command to love: 'You must love the Lord your God with all your heart, mind, soul and strength—and your neighbour as yourself.'

Stewards

God tells humanity in the creation narrative to 'subdue the earth, to till and keep it' as well as having management over it, for which we are answerable to God. In other words humankind has been given a role in this environment, the role of steward. A steward, by definition, is someone who looks after property for someone else. He has no legal claims on it, but he is in charge and answerable to the owner. So it is with humanity. We have no right to act arrogantly or independently. 'All things are put under his feet', as the Psalmist declares, but this should not encourage a go-it-alone policy.

On the contrary, the Old Testament assumes a 'symbiosis' of all living things: the whole creation working harmoniously together, to the advantage of each component part. In the laws of Israel a foremost human duty was to respect creation and submit to its rhythm and order. Indeed, the attitude to life in this part of the Bible is full of joy, encouraging the people to rejoice in nature's bounty as a token of God's love.

This somewhat idyllic picture is not so easy to recognize today, because of the highly complex industrial societies in which many people live. Our environment is the raw material for our prosperity, but it is not a limitless treasure trove. We are finding to our cost that future generations face the prospect of a bankrupt and exhausted world. A great deal of the blame for this must be placed at the door of our own generation for acting irresponsibly and selfishly towards the world's natural resources.

The problems facing humanity are immense. A Christian contribution is not only possible but necessary. The most relevant biblical concept is our answerability to the Creator. Sin warps our understanding of our role and place in creation and leads us to search for satisfaction in ourselves and our own achievements. So we sink into **relativism** ('there are no absolute standards'), **individualism** ('I matter most') and **agnosticism** ('we doubt that God exists, so we live without him'). There are two modern problems we face as we play out our role in creation:

We may overestimate our importance in the world and try to flatter ourselves that we are lords of our environment. Edmund Leach began a famous course of broadcast lectures: 'Men have become like gods. Isn't it about time that we understood our divinity? Science offers us total mastery over our environment and over our destiny. Yet instead of rejoicing we are secretly afraid.' If men and women are afraid, it may be that our nature informs us such an attitude is wrong. It certainly has practical implications: if we are lords of creation then we can do what we like with our environment. It is ours to use as we wish. When we lose sight of God, we take for ourselves a position that properly belongs to him.

The glorification of humanity can rebound upon us, so that the individual no longer matters. Often, when the dignity and glory of mankind is trumpeted, the personality and worth of the individual is brushed aside.

The classic expression of this is Aldous Huxley's *Brave New World*, in which he explores what a future would be like where our scientific achievements dominate the world. He paints a horrifying picture: genetic engineering gears what kind of people are born to social requirements, and the individual is graded according to his intelligence and usefulness to society. The state comes first and people last.

Christian teaching is bold and uncompromising. Our dignity derives from God alone. If God is, we are. If God is pushed out, we are the losers in the end.

LIFE IN RELATIONSHIP

So far we have discussed what it means to be human. But the human person can never be treated alone. We cannot survive alone, at least not for very long. Our growth as persons largely depends on the strength of the relationships which connect us with people around. Each of us is born into a family, in itself a unit of society, and we continue in different levels of community. 'People, people who need people, are the luckiest people in the world,' Barbara Streisand's song told us. Most of us are intensely aware of our need for human love and companionship.

But there is an even deeper truth about relationship. What we call 'personhood' only comes fully into being when we are in community with others. 'I', on my own am an individual. 'I', with others, am a person. This modern insight is not foreign to the Bible, which never treats the individual on his or her own. Humanity was, after all, created male and female. People need fellowship for growth to fulfil the potential within. The Bible's emphasis, especially in the Old Testament, is on 'corporate solidarity': the group is the significant unit, and it is in the network of relationships which make up the group that the individual plays his part. The creation narrative says: 'It is not good for man to be alone.'

Husband and wife
The first and most basic of all relationships is the unique pairing of husband and wife for the purpose of sharing, loving and forming new life. In the Bible sexuality is set firmly within this setting. Sex is not a thing in itself, isolated from a continuing relationship.

But Christians have not always had a positive view of sex within marriage. The church has often adopted a grudging and distasteful attitude towards our sexuality—because of the Greek influence on early Christian thought, as we have seen. The body was thought of as something inferior to the soul; it was sinful, sordid. This contrasts with the whole-hearted attitude of the opening chapters of Genesis, which portrays people most emphatically as sexual beings whose sexuality is God-given—to be enjoyed directly and properly. The fulfilment of these desires is rightly found within the unity of husband and wife in an enduring, rich and loving relationship.

What kind of partnership?
Christianity has sometimes encouraged a view of women as second-class citizens—inferior to men before God and socially unequal in the community. Even some of the greatest church fathers were guilty of this. In their eagerness to commend the advantages of chastity for

Christian ministry, they accused women of wielding a sinful and seductive influence over men. Women have even been accused of causing humanity's fall! Tertullian made a well-known attack on women: 'You are the Devil's gateway, you are the eater of the forbidden tree. You destroyed, so easily, God's image, man.' It is important to recognize the wrong assumption he makes, that women are excluded from the image of God. Humanity is the image of God, not maleness. The divine charter was: 'God created man in his own image: *male and female* created he them.'

This biblical emphasis rules out all sexist notions. There is no justification for male chauvinism. Women were not created as inferior creatures, but as people of equal standing with men and equal dignity before God. Here is a vital principle to grasp: women are spiritual beings endowed with exactly the same opportunities to find and know God as men are. The Bible never denigrates women spiritually, although not until the ministry of Jesus is the full teaching reached about their spiritual nature.

The modern movement for equality, then, has the Bible on its side. And yet it can lead us astray because of its tendency to blur the physiological and other differences that are there to see. This only makes things more difficult as we try to work out the respective roles of men and women in society. Within the marriage bond there are different roles, duties and responsibilities for each partner to perform.

This is obvious at one level: men cannot give birth nor suckle their young; women cannot give seed. But at other levels, especially in our complex society, the roles are not as clear-cut as they used to be. Modern education and social pressure have given women a freedom undreamed of twenty years ago. This is something to be deeply grateful for, yet in its turn it has its unhealthy side. The breakdown of marriages in industrial society is now a serious social problem and Christian insights into the nature of marriage are much needed.

The family

The modern family differs very strikingly from families in ancient times. We talk today about the 'nuclear' family—the somewhat isolated unit of mother, father and children. The historical reasons for this are quite well-known.

Before the Industrial Revolution, families were fairly close-knit, with the extended family of grandparents, parents and children, cousins and aunts, all living within a reasonable distance of each other. This is still a common pattern in agricultural societies. But the rise of modern industries gradually brought a change. Men and women went in search of jobs; the industrial cities, big centres of employment, attracted the homeless and jobless; the invention of the railway and the motor car increased mobility.

Today Mr and Mrs Average Family may enjoy four or five moves in a working lifetime. They will build up many important friendships along the way, while at the same time finding a gradual estrangement from their 'home' community and wider family.

It is not just parents who have found themselves adrift from their original moorings; today's children feel cut off or estranged from their parents. We call this 'the generation gap'. Again, the reasons for this are fairly clear. Families rarely seek their relaxation together; teenagers seek their amusements and friendships among their own age-group, and competing interests come into the family.

This division between the generations was not to be found in the Hebrew family. The tribe, the community, was the social context for the individual and his or her family. Great respect was given to the senior members of the family or clan, because they represented the traditions of the tribe. As 'elders' they taught the customs, folklore and religion of the group. Their experience of life and of their God was something they shared with others. Within the family children were definitely 'seen and not heard'. Respect for their seniors was drummed into them from infancy.

Children were expected to 'honour' their parents and parents were exhorted to encourage their children, bringing them up to be responsible citizens and to love God. Yet this did not result in an oppressive society. There was a delightful informality and warmth in the ancient Israelite family which saw in the network of human relationships—grandparents, parents, children, aunts and uncles and cousins—a secure refuge in a threatening and insecure world.

Two special things stand out in the biblical picture of the family:

The clan structure ensured that all groups were given a place in the family. As far as we can tell from the Old Testament, the generations were happily integrated, on the basis of the 'honour' that each had for the others.

The fifth commandment ordered: 'Honour your father and mother, that your days may be long in the land which the Lord your God has given you.' This was the Bible's standard, although like all commandments it was not always obeyed. Jacob deceived his blind father Isaac to cheat Esau of the inheritance; Absalom revolted against his father, King David, and tried to depose him; Joseph's brothers behaved in a most unbrotherly manner by selling him into slavery. But such incidents were seen as aberrations; mutual respect was still the cement of the clan.

Jewish spirituality centred on the home. The synagogue did not develop until quite late in Jewish history, and even when this became an important part of Jewish life it did not displace the family as the focus of religious life. Neither did the Temple and its sacrifices challenge the place of the home as the centre of Israel's faith.

To this day the central religious event in Judaism is the Passover, which is essentially a family event as relatives and friends gather to celebrate Israel's deliverance from Egypt. Father conducts the service with its elaborate symbolism and each member of the family plays a part in it.

The New Testament also places attention on the importance of the family. Although it lays a greater stress on the church as the centre for fellowship, teaching and service, it teaches that the relationship between parents and children is of fundamental importance. Children are to obey their parents. Parents are to be loving and encouraging, rather than repressive. It is their duty to discipline and instruct their children, showing by example the reality of faith.

The Western idea of faith as a private, individual affair is, therefore, quite unknown to Old and New Testament writers. Perhaps modern Christians can learn from the Bible that to be a member of a family is to have spiritual responsibilities towards our relatives. This is especially relevant to parents, because of the clear biblical teaching to bring up one's children to love and fear God.

No man is an island

We saw earlier that in the Bible the group is the basic unit, not the individual. We can now go a little further than that statement. In the Bible God often addresses groups and tribes as if they were individuals: 'Israel, know that I am the Lord'; 'Ephraim, I have redeemed you', and so on. God's blessings and curses on the nation affect the individuals within it. And equally what the individual does has repercussions on the whole community. When an individual sins the whole community shares his or her guilt; it affects and contaminates others. No sin is ever private; it always has a social effect.

When a couple live together without being married, it is not just their own happiness at stake; it causes uncertainty and confusion in the wider family and in the community. Marriage is not just a legal or religious ceremony. It is the public recognition of a new relationship. And God is involved, too. No relationship works as it should when his commandments are broken.

Society and its laws

As soon as communities develop, they require law. Since every community has been penetrated by sin, we need laws to protect both individuals and the group. When we do wrong, the consequences are not only penal but social, so laws are required to safeguard the interests of others.

The earliest law to be found in the Bible is the 'covenant', the agreement God made with Israel after their rescue from Egypt. It gave expression to their promise to live as the people of God—to be a distinctive, holy people. The laws which were given at that time for the life of Israel were called the 'Book of the Covenant'.

The making of the covenant was a recognition that, if a society is to work, it requires a common structure of law to give a framework for living. The absolute centre of the covenant, the Ten Commandments, crystallized the duty of God's people to 'serve God only' and honour others in the community. Jesus was later to make love the heart of the law: 'You must love God with all your heart and your neighbour as yourself.'

The covenant was produced to give a pattern for life. It is as if God says, 'You belong to me; this is how I want you to live. Pattern your life on mine.' And so the covenant reflects the character of God. When we apply this to law in the community, it is clear that we need to have laws, or guidelines, which are going to be standards, allowing us to grow into full dignity as human beings. If the laws are either too restrictive or too lax, they will restrict our development.

Law stands as a model for people when it enshrines good values and fine moral standards. But it will always remain an external standard. It cannot change us inwardly. Its enforcement may send people to prison, but it cannot make us new people with the moral ability to live well.

Paul's understanding of Old Testament law was that although it was good and honourable, in the end it condemned people as sinners. It needed the gospel to make it really effective. Only by trusting in Jesus Christ and allowing his Spirit to fill us can we experience release from guilt and have the power to live life as it was meant to be, and as the law expressed it.

THE FUTURE OF HUMANITY

The Christian view of humanity is strikingly different from secular views, because it brings God into the picture. We are not alone in an indifferent and hostile universe. We are made for a relationship with the Creator of all. This conviction has a powerful effect on the way we live now. But it also has profound implications for our future, as individuals and as a species.

We live at a point in time when many seriously question whether any worthwhile human life will continue into the next century. 'Doom' is the highlight for many pictures of the future.

In the face of this prevailing gloom, the Christian faith says confidently that this is God's world and he will maintain his control over his creation. If we abuse the stewardship we have been given, then one day God will remove it from our grasp. But that does not mean the end of God's plan for the world.

Indeed, Christians declare boldly that God is working his purposes out in creation and one day he is going to restore all things to himself. Humanity's future is but part of a bigger plan, encompassing all things. We must not be so human-centred as to imagine everything pivots on us, but rather remember that all things revolve around God.

If Christians affirm the well-being of our species within the purposes of God for all things, we also affirm the destiny of the individual. We believe it is God's wish that humanity should enjoy his presence for ever. But then what do we make of death? It cuts short our potential; it breaks our relationships; it is one of human-kind's most implacable enemies.

We may be told that biological death is an inevitable fact in a changing universe, but this does not mean it comes naturally to us. Quite the reverse in fact. It comes as an invasion of our nature, a sick joke which makes nonsense of our values, ideals and standards. Death is a limitation we cannot accept. The Bible says of God: 'You have set eternity in our hearts.' Our nature protests at something which cuts us off in midstream.

It is on this 'unfinished' aspect of our natures that the Christian faith has a great deal to share with the secular world. We are made for an eternal relationship with God. Our life in this space-time existence is limited, but for those who know God and want to share his life, there is eternity to enjoy his company. Humanity is never finished as far as God is concerned. He has plenty of time for us.

God longs for us to enjoy life of an entirely new quality and dimension. Even our best moments of experiencing God, of spiritual insight, of theological knowledge, ecstasy in prayer and so on, are but faint and fleeting foretastes of a full and lasting joy to come.

We often look at our young children, smile to see them growing up, but know how far they still have to grow before we can really call them mature. Just so God looks at us and shakes his head at the difference between today's reality and what one day will be, when all the potential of the image of God is fulfilled.

2

God the Creator

The Bible makes no attempt to prove that God exists. It takes this for granted, assuming that it is self-evident that the whole of creation displays his work. Indeed, the first thing we learn about God in the Bible is that he is the Creator who brought everything into being.

The two creation accounts in Genesis tell us two important things about God and creation. The first is that everything in creation is totally dependent on God. All life belongs to him and we can do no creative act without him. The second understanding is this: God is the sovereign Lord who is independent of everything else. He did not have to create. Then why did he?

The Bible's clear answer is that God created the universe because he loves. Creation flows from his desire to enter into a relationship of love with us all. From our own experience we can understand the link between loving and creating. Just as in a family our children are born from love and into love, so God's act of creation springs from his love which brings everything into existence.

In the first creation account (Genesis 1:1–2:4) the accent falls on the creation of all things: 'In the beginning God created the heavens and the earth.' ('Heaven and earth' is a Hebrew way of saying 'everything'.) In the next verses there follows an ascending order of creation from the most primitive creatures to God's most perfect creation—humanity. God's satisfaction at his workmanship is expressed in the statement at the conclusion of it all: 'God looked at everything he had made, and he was very pleased.'

At the heart of this story comes the creation of humanity made in 'the image and likeness of God'. This phrase tells us that there is a difference between us and other living creatures: we bear the stamp of the Creator to show that we belong to him in a very special way.

In the second account (Genesis 2:5–25) the emphasis falls on this world and on relationships between men and women. This passage develops further the high place humanity holds in creation—to 'rule' the earth as God's stewards and to have responsibility over all life.

The rest of the Bible confirms the teaching found in Genesis and develops it in four ways:

God is at work in his creation. God did not wind up the universe like a clock and leave it to tick away unattended. He is still at work in the universe, caring for it and giving it direction and purpose. So Jesus referred to this unceasing care when he said to those who complained that he healed on the sabbath: 'My Father is always working, and I too must work.' Paul echoes this by bringing Jesus Christ directly into God's creative work: through Christ all things have come into being and they are sustained by him.

God providentially cares for everything. A greatly neglected teaching these days is the doctrine of providence. This belief means that God is intimately interested in every aspect of his creation and our welfare is his delight. Jesus taught in the Sermon on the Mount that 'every hair of your head is numbered', emphasizing that God's love is careful and concerned.

We live in a sin-shot world. This world has been spoiled through sin. God created all things well but his creation has been marred and spoiled through humanity's rebellion against God. Mankind's fall into sin has affected practically every part of the created order. So Paul says: 'All of creation groans with pain . . . it waits with eager longing for God to reveal his sons.' Because we are part of this sin-shot creation we, too, carry within us the signs of its disintegration—weakness, sickness and death.

God is in control. Although the plight facing humanity is serious, God is in control. The name most constantly used of God in the Old Testament is 'Yahweh', which probably means 'I am that I am' and may be translated roughly as the 'ever-present God'.

The Bible's teaching about creation challenges much of current thinking. It reminds us that this world has meaning; if the universe came into being by chance then of course there is no basic purpose behind it, but if God created it then it has a meaning which affects all our lives. It reminds us too that God's creation is to be enjoyed. God has given it to us to take pleasure in it, to admire it and use it enthusiastically without abusing it. It also reminds us that God loves and cares for us. Our joy is his delight. Disappointment, disaster and even death cannot affect this one little bit because 'nothing will be able to separate us from the love of God'. His love is such that he longs for us to move from an appreciation of creation to a deeper acknowledgment of a Maker whose beauty and love are expressed most fully in Jesus Christ his Son.

3

A World Gone Wrong

'Sin,' declared G.K. Chesterton, 'is the most demonstrable of all Christian doctrines.' He meant that we do not need to prove the doctrine of original sin—the evidence is all around us.

The Bible teaches about sin on two different levels: original sin and individual sin.

Original sin means that when Adam fell, his act of disobedience affected the whole human race. Of course there is disagreement about just how to understand the story at the beginning of Genesis. Is it describing the fall of a real couple called Adam and Eve? Or is it rather a great poetic drama about every person's sin and guilt before God? Either way the story of Adam and Eve is a profound account of humanity's greatest tragedy—our separation from a good and holy God.

The essence of sin is brought out clearly and is made up of two parts, unbelief and pride. First of all, God's word is denied. The tempter questions, 'Has God said?' God's clear command is brushed aside through the voice of doubt. Then comes the second element in sin—pride: 'When you eat (of the fruit of that tree) you will be like God . . .' Here, then, is the irony of mankind's revolt against God. We want to break free of God and his restrictions. But we end up falling into a real bondage, one which binds our wills, our hearts and our minds.

Individual sin is the working out of this pattern in the lives of us all. Adam's sin is repeated in our own unbelief and pride. So we find ourselves daily living the tragedy of sin, wanting to be better people but failing to live up to our good intentions. First we say: 'It is so difficult to believe in God.' But what we mean most of the time is: 'I don't want to obey God's plain word to me to follow him.' Again we say: 'I don't want to be a slave to God and his out-of-date laws: I want to be free to be myself.' But we are by nature worshippers. Either we worship God or we worship false gods. Today's false gods include money, sex, prosperity and power. We extend their influence by creating pseudo-faiths such as Communism and nationalism.

Such, then, are the chains of sin. They bind so tight that no one can break free by themselves. As Jesus himself pointed out, sin is not external to us so that it can be washed away; it arises from our hearts and minds. And Paul voiced the agony of many a human heart: 'What a wretched man I am! Who will rescue me from this body of death?'

Paul, of course, answers his own question firmly and triumphantly—Jesus Christ can and will rescue us. The death of Jesus is the only place where we can find forgiveness for our sin and strength to overcome it. Only the cross can penetrate the dark and twisted pathways of our nature and free us from the power of evil.

It is easy to forget that Christ's battle against sin, the world and the devil still continues, and that we are on the front line fighting with him in the power of the cross. We live in a sin-shot world, its beauty and goodness distorted by sin and sometimes made very ugly. Political and social structures too often display sin's cancerous presence. This fact will make the mature Christian into a realist. He or she will never disregard the existence of evil: it will never stop spoiling the best human beings can do. But also the Christian will never allow sin the last word. Jesus Christ has ultimately conquered sin in his death.

4

Marriage and the Family

'Marriage,' goes the saying, 'is the nursery of heaven.' At least it is meant to be, although no one imagines that all marriages are perfect. Like every other human relationship marriage can be undermined by weakness, sin and selfishness. And if anyone is going to have an enduring relationship of love with another human being, it needs to be worked at and begun afresh every single day.

Despite the ever-increasing numbers of broken marriages, marriage is still the basic social unit in practically every society, and this was certainly God's intention from the beginning. He created humankind in his image as male and female, and it was his will that they should find fulfilment in one another. Paul even uses the loving and holy relationship between Christ and his church as a model for marriage as it should be. And Jesus treated marriage as a lifelong obligation which no one should sever. Divorce is always a terrible break in God's purposes, brought about through human weakness and sin.

But marriage is far more than the relationship of two people. It is the foundation of the family and the centre of a web of relationships which affect each person for good or ill. What does the Bible teach about a good marriage and wholesome family life?

Faithfulness and trust. In marriage there is only one

person we can give ourselves to intimately, and that is our partner. A 'holy' marriage is one in which the other person is sacred and all other men and women are 'out of bounds'. The problem today is that this clear boundary is so often transgressed, sometimes even by Christians. The main cause, as we know so well, is the power of sexual desire, to which none of us is too holy to be impervious. A couple who want to be faithful will keep the lines of communication open, building trust and helping each other to steer clear of situations which could become too difficult to handle. Also, the Bible tells us not to defraud one another in the matter of sexual intercourse. We must be willing to consider the needs of our partners and give ourselves willingly and in love, even though we may not always feel up to it. It is rare to find couples prepared to discuss this issue openly.

A disciplined framework. Love between the sexes is the seed-bed in which true love is propagated for the entire family. That love will express itself in a loving framework of life in which children will grow up to be mature adults themselves. The Bible has some down-to-earth things to say to us. Disciplining children is not always wrong: indeed, punishment appropriate to the misdeed will be necessary at times, so that children are brought up to heed what is right. Punishment which flows from love will never be harsh or cruel. Just because we are parents does not mean that we own our children: they belong to the Lord first. So Paul calls us to work at our family relationships—children to obey, and parents not to provoke or discourage.

Companionship. The good marriage and happy home is where our best friends are. In that context it should be natural to play, pray, laugh and have fun together—simply enjoying being with members of our own family. So marriage and the family, when they function at their best, can give us a foretaste of what heaven is like and of the divine family of which God the Father is the head.

5

Men and Women Together

Probably the greatest social revolution of our time has been the emancipation of women. Until this century women were limited to their three traditional strongholds: children, kitchen and church. Outside these areas women could not move without being frowned on. But now women have greater freedom and opportunity in practically every society and this has been of benefit to us all.

But there have been harmful side effects. Some feminists reject the traditional roles of women completely. Some even consider men their bitter foe. And women seem now to be at even greater risk on the streets of our cities, from violent, embittered men.

Against this background, what is the Bible's teaching about male/female relationships?

We were created equal. In God's sight, men and women have equal honour and standing. Both sexes were made in the 'image of God' and destined for an eternal relationship with our Father. This is the divine charter for human freedom and dignity.

We were created to be together. The creation story tells us that a man and a woman were not created to be separate and isolated but to be together, two beings absolutely essential and necessary to one another. Apart from one another male and female cannot *be*. We need each other not only to survive but to be truly ourselves.

We were created to be different. The desire for equality may so easily blur the significantly different things we contribute to the human family. Women and men are not the same—and the differences are far more than sexual. They include the way we perceive life, our attitudes to others, the nature of our gifts and our consciousness of sinfulness. Such differences, falsely perceived, can become points of division and bitterness. But when accepted rightly, as part of the way we complement one another, they lead to enrichment and strength.

Christians make a very important contribution to society by working out the Bible's teaching. Take, for example, the way men and women unintentionally threaten one another. Women feel hedged about by age-old traditions and attitudes, which can still make them feel oppressed in church and society. Men can find women's emancipation deeply threatening. 'Brains rather than brawn' is the currency of a modern society, and so some men feel undervalued, their strength no longer needed.

How can Christians help to confront these feelings, remove the threat and make accepting relationships possible? Even in highly developed societies women sometimes complain that they are not valued as persons by men but as sex objects, particularly at work. Directly contrary to this, the Christian message is of human dignity, treating the person of the opposite sex as a sacred person made by God for God. And the task of the Christian church is to build God's community of love in which hostility, hatred and opposition are replaced by acceptance, trust and respect.

6

Our Attitude to Money

We all need money and most people want a good income to enjoy a decent standard of living. But money in itself is not real wealth. Money is important to us because of the things it can be exchanged for—such as food, clothing and other possessions. There is very little in the way of material things that money cannot buy. And it can also give us power—power to control our own lives, and, when there is a lot of it, power over other people.

Because of the power of money there are some who regard it as evil. There is an old saying: 'Money is the root of all evil.' But this is simply not true. The Bible never condemns money. Some of its great characters— Abraham, Joseph, Job, Joseph of Arimathea—were wealthy people. What the Bible does say is that 'the *love* of money is the root of all evils'. Money itself is neutral, but selfishness and greed can make money a source of evil, with inordinate wealth for some at the expense of crippling poverty for others.

This is not all there is to be said, however. From a Christian perspective, money can be a potent force for good as well as for evil. What is a mature Christian attitude towards it?

God expects us to share our wealth and possessions. On the whole Christianity has an excellent track record on this issue. Of course there are many

Christians who have abused their wealth, but many more have given away their wealth to the poor or have diverted much of it to charitable ends. In our own day it is more crucial than ever that we share our resources with those in need. True treasure, said Jesus, is stored up in heaven and not laid up in banks or building societies. It is the wealth of love, generosity and compassion which endures for ever. Christians should be known for their radical self-giving as Jesus is remembered for his.

The Bible lays down one very clear starting-point for our giving and this is known as the 'tithe' (or tenth part). It ought to be our aim to set aside a tenth of our gross pay for God's work. This is where sacrificial giving starts.

The wealth of society should be distributed evenly. We are not supporting any particular socialist philosophy because some of these systems can be as cruel, heartless and impersonal as the capitalism they are keen to replace. A society which embraces a Christian attitude to life will want to uphold the right of every citizen to a dignified, full existence with adequate medical care, education and housing for all. Such a society will divert resources so that those in need can break out of the poverty trap.

The love of money may be a source of evil. But money can also be a tool with great potential for doing God's work. Let us use it well.

7

Justice: God's and Ours

When we look around it seems all too obvious that we live in a very unjust world. *It seems unfair* that the resources of this globe are controlled by one third of the population while the remaining two thirds live on or below the poverty line. *It seems unfair* that in most societies, East and West, there will be found the rich who own a great deal of the resources and control their distribution. *It seems unfair* that the unjust often go unpunished while the honest and deserving are harshly treated. We have to agree with the writer of Ecclesiastes: 'In this world you find wickedness where justice and right ought to be.'

But this dismal picture is inevitable only when God is left out of our reckoning. In the Bible he is the source of justice. One of the best of the many good things he has given us is a clear moral framework, by which we can live out the kind of life he wants us to enjoy. If we want to use this framework to find the way of justice, we have to focus on two qualities—holiness and love.

True holiness is based on God's holy law. 'Justice' is really a translation of the word 'righteousness'. This is a quality of life God wants from us all as we keep his commandments. But this is easier said than done. Sin is so deeply rooted in us all that we are quite unable to live this kind of life. Only by claiming in faith the forgiveness and new life which God offers us in Jesus Christ can we ever find God's righteousness.

God's law, then, cannot itself make us righteous. But still, as forgiven people, we make it our aim to live as God requires and to honour his way of living. So God's people will keep his laws and those of their society. We will honour the just claims made on us by others and try to live as honest, reliable and just people.

True justice is based on God's holy love. Christian love is not a mawkish thing but a fierce commitment to God and his world. It is a love which does more than feel sorry for the needy; it tries to do something for them. When William Wilberforce started his campaign for the abolition of slavery he was not guided by sentimentalism but by clear Christian principles of justice gleaned from the character of God's love. He knew that the gospel values every person—black and white, male and female—as of equal worth before God. He believed with all his heart that it was morally wrong for one human being to be owned by another, and he felt the scandal of one person being free to live with dignity while the other had a full human existence shut off from him. Love broke from Wilberforce as a cry for justice—a cry that spanned his whole life.

True Christianity refuses to be confined within the narrow area of life we call 'religious'. It is a way of life which spills over into our everyday experience, our social life and our political aspirations. If it is a living faith, Christianity will stand at the crossroads of human life and call people to a just God who wants everyone without exception to enjoy his bounty. His people must be committed to justice, standing up for those who are unfairly treated and courageously opposing all evil and all breaking of God's law.

PART 2

What is the Gospel?

Many people think Christianity is mainly about what we do for God. Not so. It is first and all the time about what God has done for us. That is why Christians have always spoken of the 'gospel', 'good news'—a free gift from God. This part of the book is about this gift: what God has achieved for us and how we can make it our own.

8

Good News of Freedom

A young man who had been imprisoned on many charges, including arson, burglary, grievous bodily harm and stealing, said to me in prison: 'Christ has changed my whole life. He has made a new person out of me. I know he died to set me free. I may be behind bars now, but I am free in my heart.'

This is the core of Christianity. The good news of the gospel is all about God making people whole and setting them free from prisons of sin, self, fear and death. The simple message of Christianity is that Jesus gave his life for us so that we might live.

But there is little doubt that modern people, even Christians, find the death of Jesus puzzling. His life, teaching and good works are not hard to understand, but the interpretation of his death, otherwise than as a tragedy, is very mysterious. And yet efforts to bypass the death of Jesus, or to minimize its significance, only make Jesus more of an enigma.

There are three common ways people understand what Jesus' death meant, all of them false:

It was not 'an accident'. Jesus did not die as a result of an unfortunate accident due to some misunderstanding. He was much more than simply a political pawn. The New Testament writers saw the death of Jesus as the culmination of his life and ministry. Jesus advanced purposefully towards his death.

It was not simply 'a martyrdom'. Other people have suffered worse fates than crucifixion. In Christian history, for example, followers of Jesus have died more painfully than him. Yet, they considered they were dying *for him*, in response to his love. But Jesus' death is seen in the Bible as offered for others, as really achieving something for mankind. In some ultimately unfathomable way his death gave life to men and women: his bondage sets people free, his sufferings give peace and wholeness to the world.

It was **not just 'a good example'**. Jesus' death is certainly a noble example of someone meeting death with courage and dignity. But the great emphasis of the New Testament is that here is more than a moral lesson: it is the door of God's kingdom.

Indeed his death on a cross is central to Jesus' life and teaching. Far from it being on the edge of his thought, it is at the heart of his whole teaching. His whole career only makes sense when his death is put at the centre.

WHO DIED?

You cannot understand Jesus' death unless you know who he is. A mere man cannot set people free: free, that is, of those barriers to a fully human life as children of God; free to love and live for God again.

The testimony of the Bible is that he was God's promised Son whose love took him to a lonely cross. The early Christians met a lot of mockery when they preached about Jesus' death. For the Greeks the cross was a stumbling-block, and it was foolishness to the Jews. The idea that God's chosen way of salvation was through the death of a wandering Jewish preacher and healer was outrageous.

The extent of the offence of the cross can be gauged

from something that happened in the third century, when the pagans tried to emulate the success of Christianity. They fabricated a pagan redeemer cult based on a first-century wise man called Apollonius of Tyana, for whom they mapped out a career whose main shape was based on the career of Jesus. But they missed out his death. That was too much!

Yet at the centre of Christianity is a dying Saviour who was God himself. It has always been fundamental to the Christian faith that Jesus was the unique and matchless Son of God. Only if it is the work of God himself can the death of Jesus have meaning for the entire human race.

WHY DID HE DIE?

Jesus died to save humanity. The root meaning of the verb 'to save' is 'to rescue from danger'. The danger may be physical peril, national disaster, personal danger, illness of various kinds, as well as anguish of the soul.

But there is a much deeper meaning in the verb 'to save'. In Hebrew it means: 'To make room for'; to rescue from all that constricts and imprisons, and to bring into freedom.

When people are 'rescued' they move from captivity to freedom, from darkness to light and from illness to health.

The noun 'salvation', then, is the state of being saved, and when applied to the Christian faith has a past, present and future application.

'Salvation' is located firmly in a past event. It has already happened. When Jesus Christ died, once-for-all in history, he saved us, and so we have been set free and made whole.

This salvation can be experienced in the present, through what Jesus has done, and through the presence and power of the Holy Spirit.

It will be completed in the future when God's purposes are fulfilled.

Salvation is a word which means all kinds of wholeness—personal, spiritual, corporate. But the Bible uses it to go to the very heart of the trouble, which is that humanity is separated from God through sin. When people are really conscious of their sinfulness and need, they become aware of the gulf between themselves and God. They long to be 'at one' with him. This longing is met by the Bible doctrine known as **atonement**, 'at-one-ment', the way we are put right with God.

Atonement in the Bible
Throughout the Bible we find a constantly recurring question: how can God and humanity be reconciled?

The Old Testament writers lay the basics for this question. If God is utterly holy, is it possible for sinful people to have any dealings with him? The Old Testament's answer 'yes' is rooted in its firm belief in the love of God for mankind. God has made a covenant with his people. He will not cast them away for ever.

This problem of how a holy God can be reconciled to sinful people is the reason for the God-given system of sacrifices, which were thought to 'propitiate' God and 'expiate' the sins of the people. But not everyone was satisfied that the sacrificial system was effective. The prophets were especially critical.

It was an all-too-easy way of bypassing justice. The question became more and more pressing: can anything we do bridge the gulf between holiness and sin, between God and humanity?

The New Testament answers the question simply and directly: Jesus died a sacrificial death for us all. In other words, reconciliation is central to what it means that Jesus died. All the sacrifices and ritual of the old order were abolished, as the letter to the Hebrews makes clear: 'It is impossible that the blood of bulls and goats could take away sin.' People's sins cannot be borne away by sinless animals. Yet the system did have its value. It kept alive in people's minds the connection between sin and death. Above all it foreshadowed the perfect sacrifice of Jesus.

The perfect sacrifice we could not offer for ourselves, Christ offered for us in his death. Does this characterize Jesus Christ as some third party, distinct both from God and from people, appeasing God's wrath towards mankind? Not according to the New Testament: 'God was in Christ reconciling the world to himself.' In the work of mankind's salvation the initiative is taken by God himself. The New Testament will not allow any distinction between God and Christ in what happened on the cross. Reconciliation is seen all along as something that begins from God's side.

Now we can begin to see just how radical the Christian gospel of salvation is, and why it was such a 'scandal' in the early days of Christianity. Even today it still offends people who pride themselves on their own good deeds, because it teaches certain things very clearly and simply:

We can contribute nothing to our own salvation. Our nature is so weakened by sin that we cannot rescue ourselves.

Salvation is all of 'grace'—free and undeserved. It is given, never earned.

God is personally involved in saving us. This personal action of God is summed up in Luther's phrase 'the crucified God'. God's only Son, who shares the very nature of God, became a man so that he could die for us.

HOW DID HE DIE FOR US?

The question 'how' introduces us to the theories of the atonement. Exactly what God did in the death of Jesus has been interpreted in different ways in the past. Although the church in the past has arrived at firm definitions of

56

who Jesus was, it has never yet arrived at a fixed understanding of what he did for us. No creed contains an interpretation. Christians have regarded it as self-evident that Jesus' death was utterly decisive for the needs of humanity, but it has been left to each generation to express the truth of this death in its own way.

All these different theories try to explain what it means that Jesus died 'for us'. In his fine book *Miracle on the River Kwai*, E. Gordon tells of a terrible incident in a Second World War Japanese prison camp. The British prisoners were taken back to camp at the end of a hard day's work on the Burma railway. As was customary, the shovels and tools were counted. The Commanding Officer was told that one shovel was missing. The prisoners were lined up and told to produce the missing shovel. No one moved.

The Commanding Officer ordered that a machine gun be trained on the prisoners. 'If the guilty man does not step forward, you will all be shot,' he screamed. Still no one moved. Then, as it looked as if the Commanding Officer was about to give the order to fire, one man stepped forward. He was hustled away and shot. The following day, as the tools were issued, it was found that no shovel was in fact missing; a Japanese soldier had not counted properly.

In a true sense that prisoner died for his friends. Although not guilty, he died as a true substitute; if he had not died, perhaps all of them would have.

Now clearly this can only be a faint picture of what Jesus did for us. God is no prison camp commander and we are far from innocent. Yet it raises for us an important question: How do we understand the idea of Jesus dying for us?

An objective atonement
Apart from 'moral influence' theories like Abelard's, all other theories assume that Jesus Christ's death was an

objective atonement, through which God and mankind were reconciled as otherwise they could not have been. But theologians are divided over the best way to describe how Jesus rescued us. Did he die as our 'substitute', dying a death we deserved, the innocent for the guilty? Or was he a 'representative' of the new humanity which is re-created in him as the new Adam?

The idea of Jesus as our 'substitute' has sometimes been rejected as immoral. How can we think of God, some have said, as if he would inflict retributive punishment on the humanity he created and loves? But those who argue for the substitutionary doctrine insist it is far from immoral. The Bible teaches us that God's moral law calls for sin to be punished. 'The wages of sin is death'—the spiritual death of separation from God—but our sin and guilt is expiated as God himself intervenes, through his Son, stepping into our place and dying for sinners.

The idea of Jesus as 'representative' has difficulties too. Can Jesus really be our representative when he is without sin? As has been said: 'A representative not produced by us but given to us—not chosen by us but the elect of God—is not a representative at all in the first instance, but a substitute.' But, as has been pointed out, the New Testament consistently uses a word meaning 'for, on behalf of' in this context, and avoids one meaning 'instead of'.

Yet is it really a question of 'either . . . or' with these two descriptions? Can it not be 'both . . . and'? It is surely possible to see that Jesus' death is *both substitutionary and representative*. Jesus Christ is certainly the representative of a new humanity, but he is also the one who 'becomes sin for us', who dies for the ungodly.

The mystery of the cross
In the end, when faced with the cross of Christ, we are confronted by mystery. The Bible tells us a great deal

about the death of Jesus Christ but it makes no attempt at a full and complete explanation of the reason for it. Why should God's love for us compel him to give his only Son? How can it be that Jesus was made sin for us and died in our place? How is it possible for sinful people to be counted as righteous through Jesus Christ's righteousness? How can it be that through his death our destiny is sealed in heaven?

One thing Jesus' death on the cross does make clear is that God personally takes responsibility on himself for the sin, pain, brokenness and suffering of the world, to make it new. He enters into the depths of our human suffering. Jesus takes our question on himself: 'My God, my God, why have you forsaken me?' And we can know in the depths of our need that he is alongside us; he has been there before us. He will help us through to resurrection. Despite the mystery in understanding, God does set us free.

The mystery in the cross is part of the mystery of Christianity; it should not be a stumbling-block to faith. Human life generally is shot through with mysteries. Why do people feel love for each other? It is a mystery. Yet their love is a powerful influence in their lives, affecting everything they think and do. And so it is with the cross. There is power in the cross, claims the New Testament. For those who put their trust in what Jesus did there, it becomes for them 'the power of God for salvation'.

SALVATION

We must never separate the death of Jesus from his life, resurrection and ascension. These are often spoken of together as the 'Christ events'. Although the cross is central to the New Testament, the writers did not talk about a dead saviour but a living saviour who once died. The church is built on the foundation of the cross and resurrection of Jesus. The Christians were only able to preach with such total conviction that Jesus Christ died for sinners because they believed that he was risen, and experienced that fact with intense joy.

What the resurrection means

It is one thing believing the resurrection to be a fact in history; it is quite another thing discovering what it means today. What is the inner meaning of the belief that Jesus was raised from death? The resurrection is not of someone like you or me, but of Jesus Christ who, unlike you or me, lived a special life and claimed a special relationship with God. This makes his resurrection crucial, for our salvation and for our future. The best way to find what it means is to look at four great words the New Testament links with resurrection: power, peace, joy and hope.

The resurrection shows God's power. For the first Christians the resurrection proved the claims of the crucified Jesus. He had hung upon the cross in such weakness. But in the resurrection God's power clearly broke through.

This shows us that Jesus is Lord. Peter proclaimed to the Jews gathered on the day of Pentecost: 'Listen, fellow Israelites! This Jesus ... God has raised from death ... and is the one God has made Lord and Messiah.' The resurrection proved that Jesus was all he had claimed to be and that he has a right to be called God's Son.

And so the church was born in power. The resurrection gave birth to the church. The death of a crucified carpenter could not, by itself, explain why hundreds of his followers were prepared to die for him. But after his resurrection the risen Lord Jesus promised his people that they would know the Spirit's power in a wholly new way. Even today the church is a living witness to the power of the resurrection.

The resurrection brings peace and joy. If power is the external proof of the resurrection, peace and joy are the internal confirmations of its reality. The New Testament gives Jesus' resurrection a crucial role in our salvation. 'Jesus died for our sins,' Paul wrote, 'but rose for our justification.' That is, his rising to life gives life to all who follow him. A dead saviour is no good to anyone, but Jesus is alive and through his resurrection evil is defeated. And so peace and joy come to us through what Jesus achieved.

Peace is God's legacy because sin is defeated, and **joy** floods the life of the Christian in the springing up of a new life. In his great chapter on the Christian inheritance, Romans 5, Paul brings these two words together: 'Being justified by faith we have peace with God . . . and we rejoice because of what God has done through our Lord Jesus Christ.'

The resurrection spells hope. We have the reality of Christ's power, peace and joy now, most certainly. The testimony of millions of Christians through the centuries to this fact makes an impressive story. And Jesus' resurrection has made possible more than the rebirth of the individual. It has given rise to the new community of Jesus, to a whole new humanity.

But we must not forget that our knowledge and our experience are only partial. Salvation is incomplete in this life. We know only too well that all healing is only partial and temporary; physical death is a harsh fact. We live 'in between' Christ's resurrection and the resurrection of all things.

We live in hope. But it is a hope which brightens everything that happens on earth and which gives value to every human achievement. This hope is not just for our future. God has given us a foretaste of it in the resurrection of his Son. It is God's declaration that one day we shall be as he is. So John declares: 'It is not clear what we shall become, but we know that when Christ appears we shall be like him, because we shall see him as he really is.'

Good news indeed

The gospel is good news that we are set free to be the kind of people God wishes us to be. It is good news God offers as a free gift to us who are thoroughly unworthy of his generous self-offering. Jesus' 'once-for-all' offering of himself remains valid to the present day. God will never be content with anything less than that full at-one-ment by which we are made one with God, with our neighbour, with our environment and with our own inner self. Physical health, holiness of life and social well-being make up what the Bible means by 'wholeness of salvation'.

Since good news comes to us freely and with such wonderful benefits, it is for Christian people to show forth this freedom in our lives day by day. Cardinal Suenens once told a journalist why he was so full of hope: 'I am a man of hope, not for human reasons nor from natural optimism. But because I believe the Holy Spirit is at work in the church and in the world, even where his name remains unheard. I am an optimist because I believe the Holy Spirit is the Spirit of creation. To those who welcome him he gives each day fresh freedom and a renewal of joy and hope.'

9
Finding Faith

In our modern secular world the word 'faith' arouses a great deal of scepticism, even derision. 'Faith,' said the schoolboy, 'is believing something you know isn't true.'

But faith is not credulity, believing any half-baked idea that comes along. Even secular life could not operate without faith. Someone in the office asks you for a loan of ten pounds; you lend it, secure in the knowledge that he will pay it back. That is faith. You buy a present for your husband's birthday, a watch perhaps, believing the maker's guarantee that it is reliable. That is faith.

In the Bible there is scarcely a word which has a more varied and a richer meaning than the word 'faith'. If you have faith in someone, you trust in that person's character. So, in the Bible, faith rests in the character of God. He keeps his promises to men and women; he can be trusted.

In the Old Testament the prophets spoke of the Lord's 'steadfast love', his faithfulness to his people. They may wander away from him but he remains faithful.

The basis of New Testament faith is the life, death and resurrection of Jesus. If people 'believe' in Jesus they trust in the *fact* of what Jesus has done for them. And so even faith is not the most fundamental thing in a person's salvation; what comes first is God's faithfulness, both in promise and in action. Mankind's faith is a response to God's initiative.

Trust and commitment

Especially in Paul's letters and in John's Gospel, we find that faith means trusting our whole life to God. The modern word 'commitment' comes very close to this. The New Testament seldom says merely 'believe...', but rather 'believe in' (literally 'into') God or Jesus. What is required is not just assent to an idea, but humble acceptance of what God has done.

Faith, then, is trust in what God has done, which results in a whole-hearted commitment, trusting ourselves to him. This affects every area of our life.

The Bible also makes it clear that 'faith' cannot be separated from our life, our behaviour and the world we live in. James writes that 'faith without works is dead'. But he is not contradicting the emphasis in the rest of the New Testament that we are saved by faith alone. His point is that mere intellectual belief is barren. The demons believe in God, he says, but it makes no difference to their conduct. A real faith will always issue in a changed life.

By extension we use the term 'faith' to declare what is believed. When Christians in their worship say 'this is the faith of the church', they mean the Christian faith expressed in the Bible and in the creeds of the church. The difference of emphasis between a Protestant and a Catholic understanding of 'faith' comes out here. When a Protestant uses the word 'faith', he or she normally has in mind our personal response to God. The Catholic would most naturally assume that it is the faith of the church that is being discussed, faith expressed in creeds.

In short, to have faith is to accept what God has revealed of himself in Jesus. To have faith is to yield ourselves to Jesus in the light of what he has revealed.

CONVERSION

The word 'conversion' literally means a 'turning', a 'change-over'. In Britain during the change from coal gas to natural gas, people spoke about being 'converted' to natural gas. When used of the Christian life it is associated with moving from one way of living to another, from ungodliness to holiness, from a life lived without reference to God to one which puts God at the centre.

Strangely enough, the Greek word for being converted is not used very often in the New Testament, and some have therefore wrongly assumed that the idea of conversion is insignificant. Some important questions are also asked about it:

Is conversion essential before a person can truly claim to be a Christian?

Does conversion have to be sudden?

Can a person be a Christian who has not experienced a black-and-white conversion experience but has grown into a mature acceptance of Jesus Christ?

To give a proper answer to these questions, we must look at some factors which are always present when a person comes to faith in Jesus Christ:

Awareness of need. No one comes to faith in Jesus without a sense that something is missing in life. This can take different forms with different people. One person may be conscious of moral failure, an inability to overcome temptation. Another may be aware of a sense of frustration and futility in life. Another may come to realize that life has no meaning unless God is brought into the picture. All this shows that there are many different kinds of sin, and our longing for God finds expression in very varied ways. In the Bible, Mary Magdalene's problem was different from Paul's, and Peter's was different again. But each of them saw Jesus as the answer.

Willingness to turn. The word for this is 'repentance'. The word for 'repentance' in Greek means to turn round or have a change of heart and attitude. Repentance involves being sincerely sorry for our sin and willing to change direction.

Faith in Jesus Christ. Turning is one thing, but in

itself is not enough. Many people like to turn over a new leaf, but this does not make them Christians.

Jesus called people 'to repent *and believe the gospel*'. A person must accept Jesus as who he claimed to be, the Saviour and Lord of our lives. It means taking up his yoke. By a conscious decision, I turn my back on my old life and enter a new life based on Jesus. I become a disciple, a follower of Jesus, who learns to live his way.

In the Acts of the Apostles and the teaching of Paul, the death and resurrection of Jesus are put central in Christian conversion. If Jesus died for sinners and rose to prove it, so the Christian must die to the old nature and begin afresh through the Holy Spirit.

This is expressed symbolically in baptism. Indeed, baptism in the New Testament and in the early church was in itself a symbol of conversion, in that it graphically declared a person's rejection of the old life and entry into new life through the Holy Spirit.

Looking back on the questions raised earlier, we may now be able to suggest some answers. It is clear from human experience that 'sudden' conversions are rarely sudden at all. Usually they are the result of thought and exploration which have gone on for a long time. C. S. Lewis told us that he came to belief in God on top of a double-decker bus. But this was the climax of a long, painful search.

For some, conversion is a 'crisis' event. But the experience of many Christians in all traditions of the Christian churches is that this discovery of faith may come through steady growth and teaching in the Christian life, without any crisis of belief or identifiable turning-point.

A distinction has been drawn between 'once-born' and 'twice-born' Christians. Both are valid forms of Christian experience. And yet it remains true that awareness of need, willingness to turn, and belief in Jesus are essential to Christianity itself. A person who has them all is a converted person. The route itself is not the most important thing; what really matters is the destination.

NEW BIRTH

Conversion from one point of view can be seen as our own effort to do something about our spiritual problem. We are aware, we turn, we believe. This is, of course, over-simplistic, because God too is at work at each point. But there is an element of truth in it. Because the word 'conversion' refers to the human side of becoming a Christian.

'New birth' (or, as it is sometimes called, 'regeneration') is the action of God alone. He alone, through his Spirit, gives life to those who turn to him. There cannot therefore be a true conversion without the inner renewal of the individual. My turning is met by God's gracious forgiveness of sin, and the Holy Spirit meets with my inward self.

In the Old Testament, the focus is on national renewal. The prophets realized that the many attempts to reform society had failed. Calls to repent, to turn away from evil to good living and religious observance, had all failed. A more radical way was needed. Instead of imposing the law from outside, the only real way forward was a renewal of the individual.

In the New Testament, the dominant idea is that we are so separated from God through our sin that only a birth from above can make it possible for us to enter the kingdom. Jesus' words to Nicodemus tell us that the way to spiritual life is not through religious knowledge, or through the privileges of human birth. It is the gift of God, through the Holy Spirit.

The means of new birth
A person is born again as a result of the personal activity of

God through the Holy Spirit. Jesus told Nicodemus that no one can have eternal life unless he is 'born by water and the spirit'. 'Water' refers to baptism, which will be considered later. For the moment we can say that baptism has always been seen as important in the mystery of regeneration. To be baptized, to enter the church and to be a Christian, all point to the same thing in the New Testament.

We must not fall however into the trap of thinking that baptism automatically gives new birth. Baptism is important for what its graphic symbolism bears witness to: new life in the Spirit and a decisive break with the old nature. It cannot of itself convey life in the Spirit if faith is not present. New birth means:

Death to the old life. New birth means that sin and selfishness are no longer dominant. Only a total, root-and-branch renewal can bring salvation.

The start of a new relationship. The new birth begins an essentially personal happening between God and the individual. It is a wholly new start which results in our membership of God's family.

It is the work of God himself. New birth cannot be earned or bought, only given. As the work of the Holy Spirit it is mysterious. 'The wind blows where it wishes,' said Jesus. 'It is like that with everyone who is born of the Spirit.'

The results of new birth

The New Testament speaks in unmistakable terms about the new life of the believer. He or she now has a new relationship with God as Father, Son and Holy Spirit. People who have God as their Father are taken into the wonder of a secure relationship with their heavenly Creator and Lord. Through the Spirit they are given strength to live as Christians in the world, and this ability to live as Christians will grow with time.

In Christian theology this process of growth is called

'sanctification'. Christians cannot claim to be holy, because they are only too well aware of the power of sin and temptation. What they are confident of claiming is a personal relationship with God. Their desire is to live as those who please God.

The process of growth takes place within the family of God (the church), which is the essential home for all believers. There is no such thing as a 'Robinson Crusoe' Christian; the individual Christian finds his or her life within the Christian community.

The Bible's teaching on new birth points forward to the renewed creation which is prophesied in Scripture. Jesus Christ came to renew not only the individual but also humanity and the whole of creation itself.

This new order in Christ is referred to in the Bible as a 'new creation' and even a 'new man'. These descriptions look beyond the individual and show God's intention to make for himself a new people. The new birth leads to a new hope, therefore, centred on Jesus, which affects individuals, humanity, and even creation itself.

ETERNAL LIFE

Someone once wrote on the walls of the British Museum, 'Is there intelligent life on earth?' Someone else scrawled below, 'Yes, but I'm only passing through!' We all want to know what life means and where we are going.

Humanity's most basic questions revolve around the two fundamental issues of *meaning* and *existence*, and they are closely linked together. If this life is all there is, then I may grab what meaning I can from passing moments and events, but in the end it will not amount to much. My life will pass with everything else into everlasting darkness.

The Christian conviction is that Jesus has 'passed through' and made sense of life. He has transformed our existence through his life, death and resurrection, and the new life of the Spirit that he gives to all who come to him.

The Christian has a hope, which breaks the hopelessness of existence. This hope has certain basic ingredients:

God's life transforms our existence. Our natural existence is God-given and is for us to enjoy and use properly. To live fully as human beings we need not only food, clothing and other material things, but also spiritual fulfilment. If life shrinks to enjoyment of material things only, it gives at best passing happiness. The Christian faith proclaims that in Jesus life may be lived at its highest and fullest.

Jesus is eternal life. This life is not our natural right. It is part of God's nature and can only be for us a gift. Jesus said, 'I am the life', and this is a constant New Testament theme, especially in John's Gospel. The life that Jesus gives through a relationship with him is eternal life; it is a relationship, a way of life, that reaches beyond the death of the body.

Eternal life begins now. The Pharisees believed in 'eternal' life, but it was something given to certain fortunate people after death, or at the resurrection of the body. Jesus' teaching is that eternal life begins here and now and is a present reality as well as a future hope. There is thus a continuity between life now and life to come. This life begins when a believer accepts Jesus' offer of salvation and is given the Holy Spirit, and it is deepened as the Christian encounters the risen power of his Lord.

Paul wrote from prison to the Philippian Christians: 'For me to live is Christ and to die is gain.'

Death would not introduce him to eternal life, as if for the first time, because he already knew Jesus Christ in the present. But death was a door that would usher him into unbroken fellowship with Jesus.

A Christian can be sure of eternal life. Most of us are apprehensive, about the experience of dying. But the Christian hope conquers ultimate fear. The fear of death is a paralyzing fear to modern people, who lack a sure knowledge of God, and so are agnostic about life beyond the physical realm.

Tomorrow makes a poor substitute for eternity. The New Testament speaks of the Holy Spirit being given as a 'guarantee' of our inheritance, a sort of down payment of what we will fully receive in heaven.

Through the gift of the Holy Spirit there are foretastes in our experience of our ultimate calling as children of God. These echoes include: the desire to serve God, an awareness of his presence, the overcoming of temptation through his power, the desire to worship. In these and many other ways the Holy Spirit confirms to our hearts that we are children of God. This all gives us firm ground to stand on in the uncertainties and pains of life.

Christian assurance, we must note, is not based on our own subjective experience, but on God's promise that we are sons and daughters of God. 'He who comes to me,' said Jesus, 'I will never cast away.' Though we may sometimes feel God is distant, his promise is our guarantee that he will not let us down.

JUSTIFICATION BY FAITH

In the New Testament many metaphors are used to express the reality of Christian salvation. Descriptions such as new birth, new creation, passing from darkness to light and from prison to freedom, all dramatically express the difference being a Christian makes.

One metaphor, used only by Paul, is 'justification by faith'.

The term is borrowed from the lawcourts of the first century. The judge hears an accusation against a person, and declares the accused 'justified'. 'Not guilty' or 'innocent' are simply not strong enough to express what the judge means. He is really saying, 'You stand before this court as one who is in the right.'

It is important to realize therefore that justification is not primarily a statement of a person's moral worth. It is about a person being legally in the right.

When used in a Christian sense it is a statement about our standing before God. It does not declare that we *are* righteous, but that in God's sight we are in a right relationship with him. It does not tell us how we became Christians but that we are.

How are we justified?

We need to be justified because we are in a serious position before God. We are incapable of rescuing ourselves. Salvation is only possible if it comes from God.

This is where 'grace' comes in. Grace is God's amazing love for sinners. He came to the rescue through Jesus, 'the righteous for the unrighteous'. Here we have the basis for justification: the death and resurrection of Jesus. Through his death we are released from guilt and blame and through his victory over death we are made children of God.

And so humanity has no cause to boast before God. As the hymn puts it: Nothing in my hand I bring, Simply to your cross I cling.

If grace is the foundation of justification, then surely faith is the means by which justification becomes the Christian's possession. Because of what sin is, we cannot earn salvation from it. This can only be accepted as a gift, because it is bought at the price of Jesus' death.

Where then do good deeds come in? Certainly not as a way of justifying ourselves before God. 'I go to church,' says someone, 'and do good to others. Surely these Christian things will be to my credit?' This is a very common belief. But if it were true, it would question the very point of Jesus' death. Why should God go to the extreme length of sending his Son to the cross if people are justified by their own good deeds? This is not to deny the importance of a good life, but good works are the fruit not the root of justification.

When God justifies me, he does not look at my qualities but the qualities of the one who saves me, of Jesus Christ. The Reformers used to talk of the sinner being clothed in the robe of Christ's righteousness. We are made right by his righteousness, not our own. Faith has to be seen as our simple response to an action which is all of God: a response which unites us to Jesus. We can contribute nothing to our salvation except a willingness to respond—to reach out towards the Christian life, to take it and live it in the power of the Spirit.

The result of justification

If you walk out of a court acquitted of a serious crime, you will be aware as perhaps never before of the value of freedom and the importance of your status in the eyes of everyone as a free person. Yesterday you were the accused. But now you are acquitted and exonerated of blame, free to live normally.

Now imagine your feelings if you were actually guilty of that crime but released because the judge gave you a free pardon. As an analogy it helps us to see what justification means to the Christian. We know that we deserve a guilty verdict, but that in Jesus Christ we are set unreservedly free. We are filled with gratitude for the generosity we have been shown and amazed at such love. A new life now begins—new life made possible through the Holy Spirit given to all who follow Jesus. But has our justification actually changed us inwardly?

Here we encounter a real difference of opinion between Roman Catholic and Protestant traditions. The Reformation hardened attitudes so that extreme positions were taken up. The official Roman Catholic position interpreted 'justification' as meaning 'made righteous', which, as we have seen, is not the Bible's teaching.

On the other hand, the Reformers so emphasized the objective declaration of 'not guilty' that they seemed to deny the inner reality of it, and make it a mere 'legal fiction'. This was also a wrong emphasis. Justification is clearly no fiction. It is God's declaration that the Christian is a new creation, a child of God and blessed with the presence of God in the Holy Spirit.

Justification is therefore a glorious doctrine. It takes us to the heart of the good news and is at the centre of Christian preaching. Ignore its truth and Christianity stands in danger of confusion at best and heresy at worst. Justification not only honours God's grace but also gives a proper valuation to men and women: without the death of Jesus Christ we would be helpless.

CALLING

The idea of people being 'called' by God is a great Bible theme. It is used at a number of levels:

The name by which a person is known: so Jesus was called 'Jesus' because the name means 'The Lord saves'.

A summons to a duty or responsibility. So Paul is 'called to be an apostle'; he is aware of the dignity of his office. The word is used today of some professions, and particularly of clergy and missionaries. But in fact it applies to everything God calls us to do: in work, in recreation, in marriage, in singleness—our whole life is a response to God's calling.

An invitation to something important and enjoyable.

When used of God's calling to people to receive his life, these three basic elements combine to a remarkable degree.

'Many are called,' said Jesus, 'but few are chosen.' He meant that God's invitation has to be met by our whole-hearted welcome.

God's grace is at the heart of his call. His call flows from his love for humankind. Grace then precedes all that we do, since all we can offer is our acceptance and gratitude. Grace is one of the greatest New Testament words and its root means 'to give pleasure'.

God's call is for everyone

It is a mistake to think that only some are called. The Bible tells us that the good news is for everyone and not for a chosen few; God does not bypass the vast majority of human beings. The nature of God's love is that he is merciful to us. It has been sometimes argued in the church that only the 'elect' are called to salvation (the word 'elect' means 'called'). But we need to be clear that God's love is never less than genuine. If 'God so loved the world' that Jesus died for everyone, then his call is to all people. It is never the will of God that anyone should perish.

Yet although God invites all to open their hearts to his love, he has a special desire for those who respond, that they should enter into the fullness of his call. That call is to please him in the way we live, to enjoy the privilege of Christian fellowship, the openness of his freedom, his peace—the entire inheritance of the children of God.

Our calling reminds us that life itself is impregnated with the presence of God, with his unceasing love and grace. It also reminds us that God awaits our response to his invitation to spend eternity with him. In a word, it tells us that life is a journey which will end before his throne. And then it will be made clear whether we have accepted or rejected the call of God.

BAPTISM

When the Queen launches a new ship, she says, 'May God bless her and all who sail in her.' Then she smashes a bottle of champagne against the bow.

In the marriage service, the bridegroom says 'I take you to be my wife,' and he slips a ring on the bride's finger.

When a football team score the winning goal in a cup final, the fervent supporters cheer their heads off, throw their caps in the air, jump up and down and yell, 'We've won the Cup!'

In all three, words are combined with actions, speaking with doing. The ritual, or action, gives expression to what is said.

This is what Christians mean when they talk about sacraments. The word 'sacrament' means a sign, pledge or seal. It gives expression to what is said or promised by God. Augustine said long ago about holy communion, 'Add together the word and the loaf and the sacrament is there.' Both baptism and holy communion speak of the same thing, the gospel itself. But the outward sign is different, not bread and wine but water.

Baptism in the ancient world

Our word baptism comes from the Greek word meaning to dip or immerse. Baptism as a religious rite was practised by Jews and other sects long before Christianity appeared. Jews baptized Gentiles who wanted to join the Jewish faith. It signified repentance, a change of direction.

In the Roman mystery religions, it usually meant a departure from the old life or religion and membership of a new company.

The baptism of John and Christian baptism

The baptism of John the Baptist's preaching and baptismal practices rocked the world of Judaism. His call for Jews, who claimed a special relationship with God through Abraham and whose circumcision declared their special status, to repent and be baptized caused an uproar. Especially as this rite was usually offered to the uncircumcised Gentiles.

John saw his baptism as essentially provisional. 'I baptize you with water,' he said, 'but someone is coming who ... will baptize you with the Holy Spirit.' John's baptism spoke only of forgiveness of sins. It looked forward to the coming Messiah, whose baptism would speak also of new life in the Holy Spirit.

Jesus did not baptize during his ministry. He was himself baptized by John as a sign of his identification with sinners. But after Pentecost the Christian church invited believers in Jesus to be baptized.

Peter made his appeal on the day of Pentecost: 'Each one of you must turn away from his sins and be baptized in the name of Jesus Christ... and you will receive God's gift, the Holy Spirit.' Most probably people who came forward for baptism were baptized in the name of 'the Father, the Son and the Holy Spirit', perhaps confessing that 'Jesus is Lord'. Some Christians think that baptism always involved 'total immersion' in water; others that we cannot know how much water was used.

The New Testament tells us that baptism declares four complementary truths:

Death to the old life. Water suggests the washing away of sin. Going down into the water expresses dying to the old, sinful way of living. Coming up out of the water suggests a new life with a new Master.

The gift of the Spirit. Through the Spirit, God comes to live among his people. The Spirit joins himself to those who turn to Jesus and becomes the new power for living. A Christian is a new creation.

Entry into the church. Because they belong to Jesus, Christians are members of the church, 'the body of Christ'. And so they join this fellowship of those who love Jesus. They are now committed in love and service to the Christian family.

A new covenant made with God. In the Old Testament God's covenant (or agreement) with the people was sealed in circumcision. In baptism God seals his promise of an unbreakable new covenant, based on Jesus' death for us. It is the sign to us that God's promise has been made.

10

God our Father

Words like 'mother', 'father', 'son' and 'daughter' stand for the richest relationships in human life. We are bound to our parents in a very special relationship of love. We owe them life, because without them we would not exist. But we can go much further than that: if they have been wise and good parents we can be grateful to them for bringing us up in a loving family which has helped us to develop into mature and whole people. It is against this background that we should try to understand what the Bible has to say about God being our 'Father'.

It is strange at first sight to discover that the Old Testament rarely talks about God as Father. It is the New Testament which develops this teaching and for this reason—God is only known as Father through Jesus the Son. It is a striking fact that Jesus came preaching the kingdom in which the king is a Father. Jesus spoke of his Father as 'Abba'. This is an intimate word, similar to but not the same as our word 'Daddy'. Even today in Israel you can hear small children calling out *Imma* (Mummy) and *Abba* (Daddy). By using this word Jesus was showing his own personal relationship with the Lord of all and showing that this God is not aloof and distant but close at hand. This must have seemed almost blasphemous to fellow-Jews who placed such an emphasis on God's distance from us. God's name was too sacred even to be uttered, so whenever they came upon the word 'Yahweh' in the Bible they used 'Lord'. But Jesus called him 'Father'—even 'my Abba'!

The first Christians continued this emphasis. Paul, for example, talked frequently about 'the God and Father of our Lord Jesus Christ'. It was also very natural for them to speak of God as 'Abba' because hadn't this been their Lord's practice? This awareness of God as Abba, they realized, came through lives opened by the Holy Spirit. So Paul writes: 'God has sent the Spirit of his Son into our hearts crying "Abba! Father!"'

Clearly, then, two events had to happen before God could be known as Father:

He had to come and show himself, not as a distant God, but as Father of a man who was his very dear Son. Through the ministry of Jesus of Nazareth, God is revealed as Father.

Then it has to become personal to us. We cannot enter God's family without his Holy Spirit entering our lives and starting the new creation within us. This is what Jesus meant when he said to the Jewish rabbi Nicodemus: 'Unless a man is born of water and the Spirit he cannot enter the kingdom of God.' 'Water' here stands for baptism, the outward symbol of belonging to the family, and 'Spirit' means the working of God in our lives bringing us to faith.

It is important to note that when we call God 'Father' we are not suggesting that he is masculine in our understanding of sexuality. God's nature embraces qualities which belong to both male and female natures and the Bible does not shrink from speaking of God's maternal care and love. What the term 'Father' means is that God looks after us as a real parent should. He provides for us, he defends us, he loves us. We should not hesitate to use such a term for God when it was so important to Jesus and handed on to us from him.

In our anonymous world where people are often fearful

and insecure, the doctrine of God as Father is exciting and inexhaustible. Jesus lived life aware and confident that he could not drift from his Father's care and love. We must be careful not to pray 'Our Father' and live as though we are orphans.

11

A Covenant with God

Covenant is the Bible's word for an 'agreement'. When we make agreements today—legal, social or personal ones—we seal them in a variety of ways with a legal document, a certificate, a wedding-ring, or even a kiss.

In the Bible four covenants with mankind are mentioned:

The covenant with Noah. Following the great flood, God promised humanity that he would always be faithful. The rainbow was the sign of this covenant.

The covenant with Abraham. Abraham's trusting faith, which made him risk everything on God's promise, was rewarded by God's covenant. God declared that he would make of Abraham's descendants a great nation. The sealing of this covenant was in the act of circumcision.

The covenant with Moses. This covenant sprang from God delivering his people from Egypt. He led them out of captivity through his servant Moses and revealed his name 'Yahweh' to them. In this covenant God declared: 'You are now my people and belong to me. You must be holy as I am holy.' At Mount Sinai the covenant was sealed on two sides. On God's side there came the gift of his law, given so that it might be the framework for life. 'Abide by these rules,' said Yahweh, 'keep them faithfully and you will honour me and be my delight.' On their part, the Israelites promised to keep these laws and to have no other gods but Yahweh.

The new covenant. The tragedy of Israel was that they failed to keep God's covenant. In spite of God's many appeals through prophets and leaders, his agreement with Moses was repeatedly broken. The later prophets began to see that the sinfulness and weakness of humanity made it impossible for people to keep their end of the bargain. Through them God began to show that he would introduce a new and everlasting covenant: not an external but an internal one, that is, not written on stone tablets like the Ten Commandments, but on the very hearts of us all. More wonderfully still, it would no longer be limited to the Jews—it was to be for all people.

What the prophets awaited, Jesus fulfilled. His death was the sealing of this new agreement between God and humanity. At the very moment the lambs were being slaughtered in the temple for the Passover meal, Jesus the lamb of God sealed the new covenant with his own blood.

The covenants mentioned in the Bible show that they come from the gracious, free and generous act of God. He is utterly sure and dependable, and he longs for a people to enter fully into his love. Three aspects of his character emerge from the Bible's teaching about God's covenant. He is **Saviour**: he came to Israel's rescue through Moses, he came to our rescue through Jesus Christ. He is **Teacher**: he gave the Israelites guidelines for their relationship with him and he teaches us through his revelation in the Bible. He is **Lover**: he wants his people to love him as deeply as he loves us.

Still today God's new covenant gives meaning, hope and peace. It declares that God's everlasting agreement with us has been made and will not be broken. Whatever difficulty we face we can respond, 'God has expressed his faithfulness in the covenant and he will never let me go.'

That faithfulness was sealed through the death of Jesus—such is the nature of God's love. But the covenant is also a covenant of *grace*. Salvation cannot be earned, it is a gift—God's eternal covenant is quite unmerited on our part. All we can do is to accept it gratefully through Christ and live it daily.

12

God's Laws

Law is not a very popular word these days. In all societies law and order are under attack, and many seem to think that if we had complete freedom we would be better off.

Yet God is a great believer in law! In the Old Testament we see that, following the covenant he made with Moses, his Law (the *Torah*) was given to the people of Israel so that their lives might express that they were in fact the children of God.

It is important to remember that at the beginning the Torah was not intended to be simply a list of dos and don'ts. The Hebrew word *torah* means 'instruction' and it was intended to be a framework for life, a gift of grace so that Israel might become in conduct what they already were as the people of God. Unfortunately, such is human nature that we are apt to turn a benefit into a barrier and this happened with the Law. By the time of Jesus the Pharisees had hedged the covenant around with 613 laws which the Jews were expected to keep. Jesus condemned the legalists who had made a prison camp of God's Torah: 'The scribes and Pharisees sit on Moses' seat . . . (but) they bind heavy burdens, hard to bear, and lay them on men's shoulders.'

Jesus' own attitude to the Law is interesting. On the one hand he was prepared to ignore it and even criticize it. Yet, on the other hand, he commended it and obeyed it as having divine authority. This apparent contradiction is resolved when we understand that Jesus believed that he had come, not to condemn or abolish the Law, but to fulfil it.

Jesus fulfilled the Law firstly by showing that love is the fulfilling of the Law. Indeed, he declared the double command, to 'love the Lord your God with all your heart... soul... mind ... and your neighbour as you love yourself,' to be the perfect summary of the entire Law.

And secondly Jesus showed, by his whole life of obedience to the Father from start to finish, that this was how the genuinely human life should be lived. His death on the cross ushered in the new covenant, so the way of salvation now is not by keeping laws but by receiving God's forgiveness through Christ. He and not the Law opens the way between the Father and us.

Is the Law relevant for us today?

The Law is fulfilled in Jesus Christ but this does not mean we can pass it by. Its inadequacies are clear enough. It cannot lead a person to God, and because of its appeal to standards which are beyond us only increases our sinfulness. Nevertheless it still remains 'holy, just and good'. Although we are not bound by the 613 laws of the old Jewish tradition, and although the Old Testament ceremonial law is fulfilled in the new covenant, the essence of the moral law as expressed in the Ten Commandments must be kept by us all. We are not made Christian, of course, by keeping them. But we heed them because we *are* Christians and we want to live well for God.

The gospel cannot be properly understood as good news without the preaching of the Law. Its standard of what God requires is the backcloth against which the gospel makes sense. The church fails when it neglects God's standards of holiness, justice and love.

Paul writes of the 'natural' law written in our hearts. He means by this that those who have had no chance of responding to the gospel in this life are not condemned automatically by God. Because he is the God of mercy and love, he judges such people by what they have made of the law of conscience within.

13

The Holy Spirit

'I will not leave you comfortless. I will send to you another Comforter, who will be with you for ever.' These words of Jesus, spoken just before he died, are a fitting introduction to that divine being we call the Spirit. He comes to us through Jesus Christ, and he indwells us for ever.

Before the coming of Jesus there was no clear expression of the Spirit. The favourite Old Testament word for the Spirit is 'breath', which probably stands for the powerful energy of God in the world. As 'breath' of God he creates, inspires, gives leadership, empowers, reveals God's word and gives creative ability. The prophets herald the coming of the Messiah who will be anointed with God's Spirit, in an age when all of God's people will be visited with the Spirit of God. But throughout the Old Testament the Spirit came on people for specific tasks and for temporary periods. He did not indwell them permanently.

During the ministry of Jesus the Spirit acted in great power. The Spirit indwelt Jesus fully, and the gifts and graces in their very best were to be seen in his life. But the 'age of the Spirit' properly began when Jesus' work had been completed with his death, resurrection and ascension. Jesus, Spirit-filled, then became the giver of the Spirit. He told his disciples that he would not be leaving them alone: 'I will send to you another

Comforter, who will be with you for ever.' The Spirit came in power on the day of Pentecost, inspiring the church to proclaim the good news of the kingdom.

There are four very important truths about the Holy Spirit:

He is the Spirit of Jesus. Although the Spirit has a distinctive personality, his role is never to proclaim himself but to glorify Christ and 'floodlight' the work of Jesus. The Spirit is only satisfied when the beauty and glory of Jesus are lit up by his light. It is not surprising, then, that in the New Testament there is some overlap between the work of the Spirit and the Son—Jesus is said to indwell the Christian but so does the Spirit. This overlap, however, merely emphasizes our central point—the Spirit wants to make us more like Christ.

He is the Spirit of mission. In the Acts of the Apostles we constantly see the Holy Spirit in action guiding the church, coming in power on the apostles and indwelling all believers. He is interested in enlarging the boundaries of the Christian family and making disciples. He continues to apply the work of Jesus Christ to every new situation and every age.

He is the Spirit of the church. Without the Spirit there is no church. He who was the distinctive mark of the ministry of Jesus now fills the community of Jesus. No one can be born into God's family without him. He indwells all Christian people and he is the centre of the church's unity and the mainspring of its life.

He is the Spirit of power. The word often used of the Spirit in the New Testament gives us our word 'dynamite'. That explosive power of God is seen in the Acts of the Apostles as the apostles witness boldly to the resurrection of Christ. That self-same power is expressed through the gifts of the Spirit given to his people.

So where has that power gone today? There is, in fact, plenty of evidence throughout the world today of astonishing growth as the Spirit works among his people.

Yet there are also many weak churches and powerless Christians. Two key things should be borne in mind. First, the Spirit can be grieved by hardness of heart, by unbelief and opposition and his work may be quenched or restrained. When the church tries to operate in its own power, that is when it is most weak. Second, remember that the incarnation and the cross of Christ were apparently very weak. The Spirit does not always take us along the pathways of blessing and power. Sometimes he takes us through the valleys of suffering, opposition and struggle. We should remember that Calvary was as much a sign of power as was Pentecost.

Although no clear teaching about the person of the Spirit can be found in the Old Testament, in the New Testament he is clearly portrayed as a separate person within the Godhead. In the Acts of the Apostles the Spirit leads the church. He may be lied to, he speaks, he takes direct action. But it is in John's Gospel that the personality of the Spirit reaches its peak when he is spoken of as the one who proceeds from the Father, sent in the name of the Son. The special name John gives to the Spirit is 'Paraclete', which comes from the root 'one who gives encouragement and comfort'. This sums up his nature very well.

We should never ignore the Spirit. A Spirit-less church is worse than powerless—it is dead. On the other hand, we should never exaggerate his importance so that he overshadows the Father and the Son. The Spirit exists to give glory to the Son and it follows that a balanced Christian faith will want to rest on the whole Trinity. But we certainly need to allow the Spirit room in our lives to make us more Christ-like, and allow the Spirit room in our churches to bring new life, change and development. Clinging to church tradition is sometimes the enemy of the Holy Spirit. He is always on the move and we should not be afraid to travel light.

14
God in a Human Life

Christian doctrine uses a beautiful word to describe the meaning of Jesus: 'incarnation'. It carries the sense that God in Jesus 'took flesh' and became a human person. This great claim of Christians finds abundant support in the Bible.

The Old Testament begins with God creating humanity in his own 'image'. That is, we were meant from the start to walk with God, grow like him and share his nature. But humanity's fall into sin wrecked this relationship and introduced guilt and death. It is the unspoken assumption of the Old Testament that God had to do something about this tragic parting of ways to bring us back to himself. It looks forward to the coming of God's 'Messiah' who would deliver his people from their sins. The New Testament sees Jesus fulfilling that expectation.

The New Testament takes Jesus' humanity for granted. Although his birth was exceptional, he grew as all children do in knowledge as well as physical growth; he experienced hunger and thirst; he knew what it was to feel tired; he learned from experience; there were times when he was ignorant; and he suffered a real death. The incarnation stresses the reality of the human Jesus. William Temple used to say, 'Christianity is the most materialistic of religions', because of its central message that God has revealed himself in the human life of Jesus Christ.

But equally firmly the New Testament is clear that Jesus was more than man. The total impression of this man's life, his teaching, mighty works, deliberate death and resurrection led the first Christians to preach with great excitement that this Jesus was the 'Christ', the 'Lord', the 'promised Saviour', and even 'the image of the invisible God'. The New Testament writers are compelled, therefore, by the impact of Jesus to make the most staggering claims for him, knowing that this would infuriate the Jews and send the learned Greek philosophers into peals of laughter.

But the reality of the incarnation was unquestioned by the apostles and as they preached the good news of God's salvation through Jesus Christ they saw its effectiveness in a confident, growing church. In the words of John's Gospel, they believed firmly that the 'Word took flesh and dwelt among us'.

Why did Jesus Christ become a human being?

Because humanity's need requires a saviour. Christ did not come to us because we needed a social worker. Such was our predicament that he came 'to seek and to save the lost'. God's response to human sin was personally to intervene in our history.

Because God wanted to identify with human sorrows, joys and needs. We should never present the Christian faith as though the last week of Jesus' life was the only period that really mattered. The death and resurrection of Jesus were the climax of a life given over for us. He *lived* the cross before he died it. Incarnation therefore means that Christ has now taken our human nature into God's presence as a foretaste of the glory we shall share one day.

Because we need a model for Christian living. Jesus reveals the beauty of human nature when it is lived for the glory of God. Just as a good teacher will hold up to

91

his pupils a model of what he is trying to teach, so God declares to us through the incarnation: 'This is what is meant by the image of God. See my Son's holiness, his joy and goodness, his power and victory over sin. This was my intention for you from the beginning.' Although as far as this life is concerned we shall fall far short of the quality of Jesus' life, nevertheless we should not be afraid of following the practice of the early Christians who kept before them the inspiration of Christ's life as the way they ought to live.

15

The Death of Jesus

The question 'Why the cross?' has haunted the Christian faith from the beginning. The crucifixion was a penalty reserved for criminals, and many non-Christian writers in the first few centuries thought it was a rather sick joke that the Christians preached a crucified saviour. But in spite of the offence of the cross the New Testament and the first Christians did not shrink from declaring proudly and firmly that Jesus' death was God's chosen way of salvation.

But was the cross an accident? At what point in his life was Jesus aware of the cross? We do not know for sure, but it was after Peter had given voice to his famous confession—'You are the Christ'—that Jesus began to talk less about the kingdom and more about his death. What we can say firmly is that according to the New Testament the cross was planned in the purposes of God. God prepared it as the 'highway' home to him.

'Why did the cross have to happen? Why couldn't God just forgive us and let "bygones be bygones"?' some people ask. But mankind's situation was far too tragic for such a trivial response from God. So terrible was humanity's burden of guilt and sin that only God could mend the broken relationship and heal the hearts of us all. The incarnation means that God identified with human need and suffering, and the cross declares that God took all the sin and shame and dealt with it once and for all in Jesus' death. Paul put it this way: 'God made him who had no sin to be sin for us, so that in him we might become the righteousness of God.'

We shall never fully understand the cross in this life; at the heart of it there is mystery. But God does not require us so much to understand it as to experience it, and that is to discover its benefits. We do know this, that it is God's way of salvation and it has changed the lives of millions.

Here are some of the many different ways people have understood the cross:

Jesus our Example. For many people the death of Jesus has been an inspiring example of patient and quiet suffering in the face of overwhelming odds. We can take it as a pattern when we are suffering unjustly. In the New Testament writings Jesus' obedience, ending in his death, is marked out as an example of how Christians should react when persecuted or opposed.

Jesus our Liberator. Although for us today we know Jesus to be someone who removed the sin of the world by his death, it clearly did not have this meaning for those occupying Roman soldiers who put him to death. They saw him as a political agitator. To the Jews he was a 'messianic upstart'. His claims about the coming of his kingdom appeared to challenge the law of Moses. His final entry into Jerusalem as the crowds waved palm branches and cried 'Blessed is he who comes in the name of the Lord' was laden with symbolic meaning. Today many who are fighting oppression, injustice and poverty have taken hold of the cross of Jesus as a model of someone who fought against the forces of evil and conquered.

Jesus our Representative. A representative is someone we put into a position of power and influence to express our point of view. So this theory sees Jesus as the perfect man who stands before the Father on our behalf and represents us there. This idea is well caught in Newman's great hymn: 'A second Adam to the fight and to the rescue came.'

Jesus our Sin-bearer. A dominant view in the New Testament is that Jesus died for our sin. Many have extended this to mean that Jesus died as 'my substitute'. That is, his death was a death I deserved to die; he took my guilt and sin and nailed it to the cross so that I might be forgiven and rise to new life through him.

In these ways and more the death of Jesus has been interpreted for our time. If the resurrection is the heartbeat of the Christian faith, it must be the case that the death of Jesus is its heart. A cross-less Christianity is a cost-less Christianity and will be anaemic and insipid. An effective gospel today must present the death of Jesus confidently and clearly. It is still the way of hope, peace and eternal life.

16
The Kingdom of God

Every political organization or social group that wants to change society has its manifesto or programme. Jesus' manifesto was the 'kingdom of God'. He burst on the scene about AD30 exclaiming: 'The time is fulfilled and the kingdom of God is at hand.'

What did he mean by this? In the time of Jesus the Jews looked for God to intervene in many different ways. Some longed for a revolutionary, political leader who would overthrow the power of Rome; some looked for a period of peace and prosperity in which they could live in safety and bring up their children without fear; some longed for God to send his Chosen One to establish a kingdom for the Jews at Jerusalem.

But Jesus' idea of the kingdom was very new and very different:

The kingdom was already here. 'The kingdom of God is among you,' he said; now he had come, the kingdom was here. The mighty works he was doing were signs of the breaking in of his kingdom. To follow Jesus, therefore, meant entering his kingdom.

The 'kingdom' was the rule of God in human hearts, rather than a territory with definable borders, as the word means to us. It means people, not property: people who follow and acknowledge him as Lord. The kingdom, then, for Jesus was a spiritual rather than material reality.

The kingdom became a living reality through Jesus' death and resurrection. After Peter made his great confession that Jesus was 'the Christ, the Son of the living God', Jesus spoke less about the kingdom and more about his cross. But these are not two separate ideas. The kingdom only becomes a kingdom for us through what Jesus did on the cross. His death is the key to the kingdom, the door by which we enter.

The kingdom in its fulness is yet to come. It has come in part, but it will only fully come when Jesus Christ returns to reign. In the meantime the church—that part of God's creation which accepts his authority—must continue to preach the message of the kingdom.

It is clear from Jesus' teaching about the kingdom of God (or 'kingdom of heaven' as Matthew calls it) that he was concerned with the quality of human life. We who belong to the kingdom should show it in holy living, by expressing compassion and concern for others, by being 'salt' and 'light' in society. This will involve social and political action, although we must never fall into the trap of assuming that Jesus' kingdom is a blueprint for social change today. It is important to remember that Jesus never tried to give a clear definition of the kingdom. By teaching in parables he was disclosing a revolutionary message 'in code', so that the poor as well as the rich, the slave as well as the free, the Gentile as well as the Jew, might enter.

17

Making People Whole

Christians used often to talk about 'being saved', and others knew what they meant. Today 'salvation' has become a mainly religious word. To get a full idea of its meaning in the Bible let us use three other words instead—**deliverance, revolution, wholeness**.

Deliverance. In the Old Testament the Passover Festival stood for God's deliverance of his people from bondage in Egypt. To this day the Passover for the Jew means 'freedom' because God saved them from a desperate plight when nothing else could have helped. Many times later Israel wandered away from its God and drifted into bondage. Then, too, the people cried out for freedom.

In the time of Jesus the great longing was for deliverance from the might of Rome, and this was probably in the minds of the Jews when they greeted Jesus on Palm Sunday with the words: 'Hosanna' (meaning 'our God saves')! 'Blessed is he who comes in the name of the Lord!' No doubt many saw Jesus as the long-awaited deliverer of Israel in a political sense. Jesus rejected this interpretation because it was too narrow. He had come to set people free from everything that dehumanized them and kept them away from God.

Revolution. Jesus came preaching 'repentance' and 'the kingdom of God'. 'Repentance' means 'turning around' or turning right away from yourself to head in a completely new direction. So Jesus' call was radical. He called his first disciples away from their houses, jobs and families. When Jesus said to Zacchaeus, 'Today salvation has come to your house', he did not mean an insipid change of lifestyle. He meant revolution. Zacchaeus' whole life was now turned upside down. From God's point of view it was now the right way up.

Jesus still calls people to turn away from themselves to a lifelong discipleship in following a Lord who demands obedience and faithfulness. To say that he is 'Lord' means, in fact, that I am now his slave and anxious to please him. Christians are, therefore, 'turned-around people'. They are always undergoing conversion as they seek to follow their Lord Jesus, or, in other words, they are always entering more fully into their 'salvation'.

Wholeness. The word 'to save' in the New Testament can also mean 'to heal'. So when people asked Jesus to heal them, they were actually crying out: 'Lord, I want to be made whole.' This is at the very heart of salvation. God is not only interested in our souls, he also wants us whole in body, mind and spirit—fully human, as we were created to be.

Today many churches are rediscovering a healing ministry and praying positively for mental and bodily wholeness. But we have to recognize that even the most spectacular of modern 'healings' fall far short of the mighty works that marked the ministry of Jesus. It is important to bear in mind three things when we engage in the work of healing today. First, Jesus' healings were signs of the kingdom, to show that God has broken into this world through the work of Jesus. Modern healings cannot be signs in quite this unique way. Second, we must never separate medical from spiritual healing. Medicine and hospital care are part of God's plan for our wholeness. Third, a balanced understanding of the ministry of healing will bear in mind that salvation is never complete in this life. It looks forward to the future when God will usher in his kingdom and take up his reign. In the meantime we live in a fallen world in which sin, sickness and death are always present.

Applying these three great pictures—deliverance, revolution, wholeness—to life today we can see that 'salvation' should operate on many different levels of human experience. We get a warped idea if we limit it to just one area of life.

Salvation applies to our spiritual lives. It is deeply personal. When Jesus died and rose again, this great deliverance opened for us a new way with God. Many images of this are used in the New Testament: a person is 'born again', made a new being, made free, 'justified', or put right with God. All these rich descriptions reveal the deep change that has taken place in the life of the new Christian. According to the New Testament this salvation must be allowed to flood every area of my life through the work of the Holy Spirit so that I become a 'whole' person with a transformed mind and heart. This spiritual encounter with the living God is a revolution and should lead to 'turned-around' people.

But salvation applies to social and political life as well. Jesus preached a kingdom which was concerned with the poor, the oppressed and the despised. The good news of the gospel cannot be limited just to the individual or pushed into a future world. The Christian church striving for justice is preaching 'salvation'. The gospel cannot live happily with aspects of life which bind or grind people made in God's image.

Salvation, then, affects the whole of life. It comes from a great God whose love desires our total wholeness and complete freedom. It comes to us through Jesus, whose name means 'he who saves'.

PART 3

How Do We Live Christian Lives?

Once people have begun their lives with God, a whole new world opens up before them, with new possibilities—of prayer, of love . . . And on top of such personal discoveries, we find we have entered a new community. In this part we map just a few features of the Christian life.

18
Baptism

When a new Christian in New Testament times went down into the water of baptism, what was at stake was total commitment. This commitment was being displayed in three different ways, and it presents a challenge to us today.

In baptism God commits himself totally to us. Baptism declares God's love and grace which is expressed supremely in Jesus' life and death. His death was in fact his baptism, which opened the way of life and peace to us. Baptism declares to us that we are forgiven, that we are now God's children and that his Spirit is given to all who follow him. Baptism, therefore, says as much about God as about us; it speaks of his sacrificial love, that he will never forsake us and never let us go.

In baptism we commit ourselves totally to him. In the service of baptism the new Christian is actually stating two things. First, that he or she repents of a sinful past life and is willing to renounce it. Second, that the new owner of his or her life is now Jesus Christ. Paul links together Jesus' death and resurrection and our baptism. The new Christian, by going under the waters of baptism, enters into the death of Jesus and rises from it to share in the resurrection. Jesus' death was his baptism for us; our baptism is a death to the old life. For the New Testament Christian this was no game or play with words. To say

'Jesus is Lord', as each did at baptism, amounted to saying that from now on Jesus Christ came before everything else. They were prepared to face insults, ignominy and perhaps even death because of the love of their Lord.

In baptism the church gives itself totally to us. Baptism is not a private and personal agreement between God and us. It takes place within the family of the church, and without that family we cannot survive as Christians. We need its fellowship, its life and its help. Through his church God's grace comes to us in innumerable ways, leading us into deeper faith and commitment and on into greater maturity. When we talk about the 'sacrament' of baptism we are speaking of two things which are going on at the same time. The outward part includes such things as water, Bible readings, the minister and the congregation. The inner part is what God is doing in the sacrament through his Spirit. That part, like the seed sown in the ground, only becomes visible much later on. The classic picture of baptism is as 'new birth', and this is a reality to Christians because they are aware that through the Holy Spirit they now look at life quite differently, and belong now to a new group of people.

How far is this New Testament pattern recognizable in our practice of baptism today? This is a question to be asked both of churches that baptize infants and of those that baptize only adults. God wants not half-hearted believers, but men and women who are wholehearted and reckless in their love for him. Do our baptismal disciplines express this element of commitment? Many churches are guilty sometimes of dropping standards in their obsession to make 'more' disciples. But those who have not counted the cost will quickly fall away.

We should question as well whether our church is taking its responsibility seriously to love and care for new Christians. Just as we would question the love of a mother and father who did not bother about their children, so with a church which allows people to drift away from its

103

fellowship and is not a welcoming and accepting family. Such a church is not worthy of the trust which God has placed in it.

19

How to Pray

Most people pray. Some, it is true, only pray when they are in trouble, but statistics show that many people consider prayer important.

For the Christian, prayer is more than a religious duty—it is his or her native air, a lifeline to God with whom he or she has a permanent relationship of love. This relationship is the start of real believing prayer. Paul tells us that it is the Spirit's job to spark off this prayer life in us: 'Because you are sons, God sent the Spirit of his Son into our hearts, the Spirit who calls out, "Abba, Father!"' Because of this new relationship of children to God our 'Father', we can always come into his presence, and we know that he cares intimately for us.

Prayer takes many different forms, of course. One helpful outline of the various forms of prayer is in the letters of the word ACTS—Adoration, Confession, Thanksgiving, Supplication (that is, asking).

But fundamental to prayer is conversation. Just as chatter, laughter, talking and asking is the life-blood of normal conversation in any family, so God is anxious for us to speak to him and for this conversation to be as natural as breathing. And God is not the slightest bit interested in the type of language we use when we talk to him. He does not demand liturgical or religious expressions, and he does not pick us up when we make grammatical errors!

Because prayer is heart-to-heart sharing with someone we love, we should use language which comes naturally to us.

'Lord, teach us to pray,' asked the disciples. Jesus replied by reciting the Lord's Prayer, more or less implying, 'This should be your pattern.' This great prayer breaks down into seven petitions:

The first three are concerned with God's glory—'hallowed be thy name . . .', 'thy kingdom come . . .', 'thy will be done . . .'

The next three are to do with our needs—'give us . . .', 'forgive us . . .', 'protect us . . .'

Finally we come back to God's glory—'thine is the kingdom . . .'

Here, then, is the Jesus dimension in prayer. It is all too easy to begin with ourselves and our needs, but Jesus commands us to begin with God and his honour. He who taught us to say 'Our Father' is the one who knows that we may rely on God with utter confidence.

But why do we pray? If God is a loving Father, why do we need to go to him with a begging bowl? Yet look at the example of Jesus. He told his disciples, 'Ask, seek, knock,' but just before he had said about human needs: 'Your Father in heaven knows that you need them.' He saw no contradiction between the two things, possibly because prayer is much more than asking God for help. In prayer we enter into his concerns for the world, for others as well as for ourselves. It is a dynamic engagement with the resources of God, not twisting the arm of a reluctant God, but joining in God's spiritual battle against all forces which oppose his kingdom. God will expect us, therefore, to go to him with all our burdens and needs because that is what it means to belong to a family.

And will he give us what we want? God will always hear our prayers—of that we can be sure. But his response will not always be in accord with what we want or when we want it. Because he is the sovereign Lord of all, we must leave him to respond 'according to his will'.

We have said that most people pray. But, to God's great sorrow, and our impoverishment, most of us are mere novices when it comes to prayer. We paddle in the shallows of a relationship with God, when he longs for us to enter into the depths of a vibrant and rich prayer fellowship with him. For that to happen we need to spend time in his presence, just resting, contemplating, questioning, seeking—and finding.

In this, as in any great enterprise, we shall need the help and advice of counsellors and spiritual giants who know more about depths of prayer than we do. These days there are many sources we can go to. Because prayer is power, God wants to raise up 'prayer warriors' so that they may join him in the spiritual battle against all that opposes his will.

20
Worshipping God

To worship means 'to give God honour' and acknowledge his worth. When we worship, then, we are more or less saying to God: 'Thank you for all you have done for us and given us. Help us to put you first in our daily lives.'

The first Christians were Jews and used to worshipping the God of all creation. But so great was the impact of Jesus Christ on their lives that he turned upside down their understanding of worship, so that he himself became the centre of their worship, along with the Father and the Spirit. Prayer was offered in the name of Jesus and hymns sung in his honour. For example, the famous description of Christ in Paul's letter to the Philippians was almost certainly an early Christian hymn and one well known to Paul's readers. At their baptism, Christians declared 'Jesus is Lord' and so made clear the centrality of Jesus in worship.

The focal point of worship in the New Testament is the Lord's Supper or 'Eucharist' ('thanksgiving meal').

Worship is our response to what God has done and continues to do. But we must work out in our own culture just how worship is to be carried out, applying principles of New Testament insight.

Is worship to be formal or informal? The church of the New Testament had no developed forms of ministry or worship. To judge from Paul's first letter to the Corinthian church, worship was largely improvised with a great deal of freedom of expression and with a vivid awareness of the presence of the Spirit in power. Paul's letter shows that he was not altogether happy with complete spontaneity which, instead of leading to real 'Spirit-freedom', resulted in bondage for many. He gently suggests some controls so that all the Christians might feel equally at home.

The Bible gives no norms for worship, which varied according to place and culture. And so surely we should be extremely careful about expressing judgments as to whether any particular style of worship is 'right' or 'wrong'. In our own day some prefer their worship to be offered with full and rich ceremonial—with choirs, processions, vestments and with other ritual forms. Others, however, like it plain with the minimum of fuss, with lots of participation, hearty singing and, perhaps, even with the raising of hands in adoration. Both styles are correct according to the needs of the worshippers, realizing that temperament and culture are important factors to be considered. Some cultures will want it 'high and hazy', other cultures 'low and lazy'. What is important is that our worship should be relevant to the congregation and its culture—otherwise it will not be authentic.

What importance have buildings? Christianity began as a non-religious type of faith. Because Jesus had brought a complete salvation and opened the door to the Father, Christians had no need for the temple, a sacrificing priesthood or even religious buildings! Because the first Christians did not conform to contemporary religious ideas they were called 'atheists'! It is a sad irony today that people outside the church identify a congregation by a building rather than by a people.

Now buildings clearly help. To have a base, a home which the family may adapt to express a living faith and where others can be brought in is, of course, nothing but gain. But buildings can also become snares and hindrances. We may end up caring more for the building than the gospel and more for our traditions than the Lord of the traditions. We are called not to be museum-tenders but a people willing to share our faith in a living Lord.

What makes living worship? Just as there are no hard and fast laws about the structure of worship, so there are no laws as to what must be included. Certain elements, however, stand out in New Testament church life and demand attention. The first Christians worshipped with grateful and joyful hearts. No one could accuse them of dullness! Paul writes: 'Sing psalms, hymns and sacred songs; sing to God with thanksgiving in your hearts.' Should not joy and praise be a fixed feature in our worship too?

Then again, receiving instruction in the faith appears to have been another important ingredient. This would account for the emphasis placed on teachers and prophets in the early church. Their role was to build up the congregation through their ministry. So today, a church which neglects instruction and sound learning will produce immature and weak Christians. Another element would have been prayers of intercession and confession.

But without any question, the pinnacle of praise and adoration would have been when the New Testament Christians broke bread together and celebrated their 'eucharist'.

Let us note, finally, a refreshingly relaxed and unfussed air about the New Testament approach to worship. It was their love-response to Jesus, and love cannot be bound with rules and regulations.

21
What is the Church for?

'For we are an Easter people and Hallelujah is our song,' said Pope John Paul II, and it is not a bad definition of what Jesus intended the church to be. Its bedrock is the resurrection and its message is one of joy.

Unfortunately, the church has not always expressed these things in its life. The established churches have often stood in the way of people reaching Jesus Christ. Yet at its best the church is something great. Four New Testament images give a clear picture of what God wants his people to be:

The church is the people of God. Israel was originally chosen to be God's people and his witness to the nations. Then through Jesus a new way was opened up, and because of his life, death and resurrection all who follow him are now the 'people of God'. They are people of faith, trusting the promises of God.

But was it Jesus' intention to found a church? There can be little doubt that it was. He called twelve apostles around him, and sent them out to make disciples and to proclaim the message of the kingdom. His last act was to tell his followers to go and tell others. According to Matthew, Jesus said to Peter: 'You are Peter and on this rock I will build my church.' A new people was to grow from Jesus' ministry. Either Peter's confession or Peter himself was to be the starting-point of the people of God.

The church is the body of Christ. Paul was the first to use this phrase of the church, and no one knows for certain where he got the idea from. It could have simply been taken from the notion of the human body with each limb and organ having its own function. If so, it is a beautiful picture of each person serving Christ joyfully, gladly and wholeheartedly. Whoever we are we matter to the body, which is the poorer for us not being there.

On the other hand, Paul may have taken the expression from Jesus' words at the Last Supper, 'This is my body.' If so, he is stressing the church's mission to continue the teaching and ministry of Jesus. It exists to be his body in the world; healing, helping, sharing and uniting. The two sacraments Jesus gave us express the meaning of the body, too. Through baptism we join it; through holy communion we are nourished in it.

The church is the temple of the Holy Spirit. This rich description speaks of the presence of God's Spirit in and among his people. Each individual Christian is filled with God's Spirit and so is the whole body. He is given to us to make us 'holy' and powerful. Although it is possible to 'quench' the Spirit and 'grieve' him, the Spirit of God is active within the church and working through it. The growth of the church is a tribute to his work.

The church is the bride of Christ. This metaphor, found in the writings of Paul and in Revelation, looks ahead to the future when at Christ's coming the church will be presented to the bridegroom as a glorious and pure bride. In that day all its imperfections will be removed and it will be a fitting partner for God himself. Wherever it is placed, God's church lives within the dynamic tension between what it is and what it ought to be. The **people of God** should live more like him, the **body** must continue to grow, the **temple** has still to be built and the **bride** awaits the call of the bridegroom.

Three dangers continue to dog the church's story. One such danger is exclusivism—that my church is the only true church. But the church belongs not to us but to Jesus Christ and those who confess him belong to it regardless of denominational tag. Another is tradition. Church tradition is often a great blessing but it may also silt up the channel of God's grace if it is valued above the message of the cross. And a third danger is organization. The church began as an 'organism', like a plant adapting to its environment and new situation. Inevitably, organization began to shape and direct the spontaneous ministries which sprang up. But when a church is over-organized the creative work of the Holy Spirit may be squeezed out and the gifts of God's people may not find expression. Only a church alive to the Holy Spirit will express the joy of the resurrection.

22
Gifts of the Spirit

The first gift the Christian receives is the gift of the Holy Spirit. He comes to every Christian who opens his or her life to Jesus Christ. He works in our lives, deepening our love for Jesus, and honing our abilities and gifts in his service.

The clearest teaching about the gifts of the Holy Spirit is found in 1 Corinthians 12, but there are also lists in Romans 12, Ephesians 4, and 1 Peter 4. The church of Corinth had a problem, one stemming from their very success. To their great joy they found that their faith actually worked! Things started to happen. There were those who discovered that they had gifts of healing, prophecy, teaching, miracle-working, tongues-speaking, leadership and so on. So great was the Spirit's generosity that his 'anointing' came on many in the fellowship. But instead of these wonderful experiences leading to greater service for Christ and deeper humility, those who received gifts used them to boost themselves, with the result that selfishness, pride and envy began to split the fellowship open. Paul has to remind them strongly that gifts are given by God—Father, Son and Spirit—and they do not originate from us. And they are to be used for one another, the limbs and organs in a single body.

Paul makes no tidy classification of the gifts. But for the sake of convenience they can be separated into two kinds:

Speaking gifts. Among other gifts of speech, Paul mentions teaching, speaking in tongues and prophecy, which are gifts fit to be used in the congregation. 'Tongues' is a gift which has perplexed many. It seems to be a special language given to individuals for praise, worship and strengthening. Sometimes it bubbles forth in ecstatic utterances. Paul does not deprecate the gift but he does deplore people using it for their own sake. He therefore instructs that when it is used in the congregation it must be interpreted. 'Prophecy' is not another form of preaching but, more probably, a special message from God about the spiritual needs of the congregation.

Action gifts. Paul mentions a number of gifts which are also channels of the Spirit's power but where the emphasis falls on what is done rather than on what is said: healing, miracle-working, helping others and even administration.

The rich abundance of divine gifts which flowered in such variety in Corinth is testimony to the gracious activity of the Spirit, but it would be unwise to expect their experience to be reproduced in exactly the same form today. 'The Spirit blows where he wills,' and refuses to be confined to what we expect. Yet still he gives gifts which match our needs today.

It is just as important for us as for the Corinthians to heed the controls that Paul set around the use of the gifts in the congregation.

First, they were to be used to build up others. The purpose of spiritual gifts is service. Paul rebukes those 'speakers-in-tongues' whose enthusiasm was hindering the church. We, too, should be cautious of any gift which appears to divide the congregation or exalt the user. We will want to ask: Does this gift build up the life of our church?

Next comes the principle of love. The gifts will pass away when their work is done, but love lasts for ever.

What is more, Paul argues, without love to guide and control, spiritual gifts have no more value than the noise of a clanging gong. Alongside his teaching about spiritual gifts, Paul sets a most wonderful passage on the nature of Christian love. Some have suggested that it is modelled on the person and work of Jesus Christ, in whom we find that perfect balance of giftedness and sacrificial love.

And another essential control in the use of gifts is that of order. Paul does not want to freeze out any genuine gift; rather, he wants them to flourish within an ordered spiritual quietness in the fellowship. Speaking in tongues, prophecy and other expressions of the Spirit's activity are still allowed in worship, but Paul brings them under sensible control so that all may benefit.

And what about the church we attend? Our situation may be the opposite of that of the church at Corinth. Instead of the Spirit working in profusion there may be deadness, dull order instead of spontaneity, apathy instead of eager expectancy. The Holy Spirit never gives up on the church, and we should never cease to love, pray and hope that God's gifts may flourish in abundance where we are.

23
God's Servants

We often speak of 'the church's ministry', as if this meant only clergy and full-timers. But 'ministry' simply means 'service'. Ministry begins when people start to follow Jesus Christ. It is the hallmark of discipleship: to be a follower is to serve.

When the first disciples started to follow Jesus he soon got them to work learning and doing. They entered into his ministry of proclaiming the kingdom just as we also, when we serve others, enter into it. At the heart of the New Testament is this conviction that since Pentecost, when the Spirit came on the waiting disciples, all Christians have gifts and talents to offer their Lord and one another. So important is this point that we can put it this way: the church is ministry.

The whole church is to be a 'royal priesthood'. Although there is only one true priest—Jesus Christ, who died a sacrificial death for us all—the church took over Israel's priestly role of representing God to the world. Yet still there are distinctive ministries which God gives to his people within the wider ministry of the church.

The first ministry we see in the New Testament is that of the 'Twelve', probably to be identified with the apostles. Their identity came from having been with Jesus in his earthly life and witnessed his resurrection.

After Pentecost, ministry arose very naturally according to what was needed and as the Spirit poured out his varied gifts. Many of the terms used arise from the nature of the task—the teacher, the prophet, the deacon, the healer, the interpreter and even the word 'bishop' which means 'overseer'.

No single authorized order of ministry arose in the New Testament. There seem to have been many different patterns of ministry. It was only after the New Testament period that a threefold order emerged—bishop, presbyter (or 'elder') and deacon.

We need to pick out three essential jobs which Christian ministry at its best will perform:

Authority. It is very important for the sake of the body that we obey those who are set over us in the Lord. Although Paul teaches that every Christian is a 'minister', yet he urges obedience to those ministers who have been given authority and that we should recognize clearly their role to lead and guide the church. This is a very important principle for the church today when there are some who think they have the right to depart from the teaching of their churches and found new ones.

Service. We have no gifts which are just for us. Ministry is never for ourselves but always for others. Jesus showed us the example by taking a towel and washing the feet of others. Whether it is our lot to preach to thousands or to work as a porter in a hospital, all ministry for Jesus is sacrificial. It is often unrewarding and humdrum, and sometimes its consequences can be painful and costly. But for the Christian it is always worthwhile.

Building up. Because the church belongs to Jesus Christ, those who have special ministries within the body have a duty to build it up to please him. This happens when there is effective leadership—a growing church will have leaders with vision and clear goals. Gifted teaching also plays an important part, since it is through steady proclamation of the faith that people grow from immaturity to a mature and adult understanding.

But the sacraments also help this process of building up. The first, **baptism**, is a once-for-all sign of new birth. It is an essential mark of belonging to Jesus. Although it has always been normal practice for this sacrament to be administered by a lawfully-appointed minister, in fact any Christian can baptize if given that responsibility. And the second sacrament, **holy communion**, was intended to be taken repeatedly as a sign of nourishment. From earliest times the leader of this 'meal' was someone authorized by the body to celebrate the feast on their behalf. It has been common since about the third century to call this celebrant a 'priest'. This word is not acceptable to all Christians, as to some it seems to imply that Christ's work on the cross was somehow not complete. Others are happy with it as long as it merely indicates that the 'priest' is representing the priesthood of the whole body.

The Bible's teaching reminds us that we are engaged in ministry whatever we do—whether we work in the church or in the world. Ministry does not belong only to a special group but to us all. Nevertheless, God does call people to special functions within the body and we should all be alert to the challenge to take up new tasks for him and to use our talents in his service.

24
Sent by God

David Livingstone, the famous Scottish missionary-explorer of the last century, was once asked why he chose to be a missionary. 'God had only one Son,' he said, 'and he was a missionary.' It was that fact that made him choose his career.

Mission in fact starts and ends with God. The Bible makes it clear that he is a 'sending' God. He loves his world so much that in spite of our sin and weakness he sent his messengers, he sent his prophets, and finally he sent his Son to establish his kingdom. The entire activity of God in creation and salvation has a mission aspect to it because God's concern flows from his love. He loves us too much to leave us where we are.

Three important truths about mission need to be understood:

Mission is God's work. It is a mistake to begin with the church. Mission springs from the love of the Father, is given practical expression in the work of the Son and is made effective through the ministry of the Holy Spirit. It is God's outgoing love for the whole of creation, God's work in God's world.

Mission is God's care for the whole of life. The good news which Christ came to share embraces the whole of reality and takes in not only preaching good news to those who are in spiritual need (evangelism) but also caring for the poor, the needy and oppressed. Mission which stops at the doors of the church is defective, because God's mission is world-centred and not merely church-centred. Indeed the Bible's order of things has God moving out to the world before he moves out to the church.

Mission is God's people caring for God's world. Because God cares, we care. Because his love has been poured into our hearts, it overflows into his world. Pentecost is the great symbol of this. The gift of the Holy Spirit not only created the church, it made all Christians missionaries and we are all involved in the task of mission.

One way we do this is by simply *being who we are*. The key word is 'presence'. Just as Jesus brought in the kingdom by living among people and showing the compassion of God, so the Christian, by being with others, can bring the presence of Jesus and show his love and goodness.

Another way is by *sharing what we have*. Someone once defined evangelism as 'one beggar telling another beggar where to find bread'. In the task of evangelism we simply share what Jesus Christ means to us and has done for us. It may not be our gift to preach or explain the intellectual dimensions of the Christian faith, but every Christian can tell his or her own story of what God has done and is continuing to do.

And yet another way is by *serving others*. Just as Jesus came to serve, so the Christian gospel becomes good news for people when it is expressed not only in words but also in loving action and service.

'Go into the world and preach the gospel,' said Jesus, and this is still the church's charter. This makes missionary congregations of Christian churches—being, sharing and serving. A church begins to grow when it turns its attention outwards to the world. But that movement away from its own life and concerns may be the pathway into pain, challenge and crisis because it is the movement of the cross. But remember mission ends with God as well as beginning with him. And so we have every confidence that God's purposes are being worked out.

PART 4

How Can We Understand the Bible?

Christians believe that their faith is not a clever human invention; God has made it known to us. He has shown us what he is like and what his purpose is for humanity. And we can trace this revelation in the Bible. This means it is crucially important that we understand what the Bible really is and how we can read it with understanding. This last main part aims to help us know and love this book of books.

25

How Can We Understand the Bible?

'The Bible is like a wide river in which lambs may splash in the shallows and elephants may swim to their hearts' content.' So said Pope Gregory the Great long ago, and he was quite right. The Bible does indeed have the resources to feed the most junior disciple and nourish the greatest saint.

But the Bible, like a great river, is rather forbidding at first glance. We find ourselves asking: How do I get into it? How may I understand the different parts of this vast book? Are there basic principles to guide me?

WHAT KIND OF WRITING?

The Bible has a very complex history that arches over more than a thousand years, culminating in the story of the growing Christian church. It is more a library than one single book. In fact, it consists of sixty-six books containing many different types of literature.

Clearly, then, our understanding of what we read will depend on what type of book or writing it is. For example, when we are reading a psalm, we should bear in mind that the Psalms are a body of spiritual literature with human emotions of anger, despair, hope and faith expressing the honest feelings of the people of God. It is not surprising that millions of people have found the Psalms a wonderful vehicle for worship and faith. Many depressed people have found the words of Psalm 38 fitting their own feelings exactly, and without having to find words of their own have used its language to speak to God: 'I am worn out and utterly crushed; my heart is troubled, and I groan with pain. O Lord, you know what I long for; you hear all my groans.' Or if you are bursting with joy and happiness, try the splendid words of Psalm 98: 'Sing a new song to the Lord; he has done wonderful things! Sing for joy to the Lord, all the earth!' But it would be a mistake to build up carefully constructed doctrines from the Psalms, because that is not their purpose.

Similarly, the history books and stories should be interpreted according to their own categories and not pushed beyond the obvious meaning they convey. So before we attempt to find spiritual meanings in the text we will first want to know what would have been the original meaning had we been living at the time. The same will be true of the prophetic books; it helps a lot to know the background, and where each prophet fits in the history told in Kings and Chronicles.

The Gospels are a particular kind of history, focused entirely on understanding the meaning of Jesus' life, teaching, death and resurrection. And the letters, again, will become much more meaningful to us if we can see how they fit into the story of the early Christians, part of which we can read in the Acts of the Apostles.

APPLYING THE BIBLE TO OUR LIVES

What steps must we take to get from a first reading of a Bible passage to making what we read practically helpful in our daily lives?

First, put the passage in its context. What happens before and after these verses? What else does the Bible tell us about these people, or about this particular belief?

Next, look at the main characters and the significance of what they are saying.

Then try to draw out the central teaching of the passage.

Finally, we need to go on and apply the story to our particular situation.

Unless we find some practical help in a Bible passage, we have not fully understood it. The Bible is God's message to us, intended to shape our living and thinking. How many of us have said after a difficult or painful situation, 'I have to admit that I did not call upon the resources of the Bible then'?

We need to carry our daily Bible reading into our daily life. Take the many stories in the Gospels about being a disciple of Jesus. In whatever situation today—at home, at school, at work, or wherever—I must constantly ask what it means to be a disciple of Jesus there. Does it show in my thoughtfulness towards others; my speech and attitudes; the character of my life?

We can also draw strength from the Bible in the problems and situations we enter. How do we face unemployment, severe illness, the prospect of dying, anxiety about members of our own families? At such times the Bible is a wonderful comfort, support and strength because it brings to us all the resources of God himself.

A very good friend of mine, Joan, died last year of cancer. Her attitude towards her own death was an inspiration to us all. Her secret was that she took the Bible at its word. She trusted in Jesus, applied the rich message of the Bible to her daily life and was not found wanting when she had to face up to her own death.

Another friend, John, has been a Christian for only four years and last year he was made redundant. He had no job to go to and he experienced the soul-destroying experience of searching for work without success. But from the first he said, 'God is my heavenly Father. He will not fail me. I will continue to trust him and I know that something will turn up.' But for months nothing did turn up and when it did the job was not as well paid as his previous one. A particular passage that helped John was Matthew chapter 6 verses 31 to 33. 'Jesus said, "Do not worry, saying, 'What shall we eat?' or 'What shall we drink?' . . . your heavenly Father knows that you need them. But seek first his kingdom and his righteousness, and all these things will be given to you as well." ' John made this passage his armour and clung to it when things were tough and he and his wife got discouraged. His testimony today is that God carried him through, and his faith grew stronger and more confident.

It helps if we listen to what God is saying through others. We cannot live the Christian life on our own; we need Christian fellowship, which is where the church comes in. It often helps to read a Bible passage with Christian friends, who can each bring their own encouragement, experience and insights to one another. God often uses the sermon in church, too, to encourage and challenge. So listen carefully, asking in prayer beforehand, 'Is there a special word for me in this address?'

There are some practical tips which will help us grow in understanding and applying the Bible. A good translation with clear print is essential. There are many excellent versions on the market these days and it may be advisable to get the advice of a pastor before buying a Bible. Once you have decided on a certain version, it is worth sticking with it. Also, it is important to be regular in our reading. Better a little study regularly than an enormous and impressive onslaught once a month.

The message of the Bible is as vital today as when it was first written. It is worth becoming practised and skilled at understanding what the Bible means.

26

The Book of Books

Christians regard the Bible as uniquely inspired by God. But others, not Christian, also set a high value on this book. Thomas Huxley, a nineteenth-century agnostic and evolutionary pioneer, said of the Bible: 'This book has been woven into the life of all that is best and noblest in Western civilization.' Of course the language of the Bible has penetrated Western culture, but Huxley meant more than that. The Bible has changed the lives of countless individuals, and through them has had a profound influence for good on our moral and cultural life. This influence now spreads out far beyond the West.

Where has this unique power come from? All Christian churches agree that the Bible is inspired by God and authoritative for life and belief. Why?

We must begin with the book itself. The Bible we hold in our hands is really a library of books—thirty-nine in the Old Testament and twenty-seven in the New. (Strictly speaking we should be calling them Old and New Covenants rather than Testaments.) The first part—the Covenant, or 'agreement', God made with the Israelites—is the Bible of the Jews. Only the second part can be called 'Christian' in the fullest sense, because these books were written by convinced Christians.

It is a matter of resentment among many Jews that the Christian church has taken over their sacred writings and made them part of our 'canon', or list of inspired books. But the remarkable process by which this took place began entirely through the impact of Jesus Christ. The whole Bible clusters around him and we must go back to his life, death and resurrection to trace those steps which led to the Bible acquiring the authority it has today.

JESUS AND THE BIBLE

Jesus was a Jew, of the tribe of Benjamin and of the house of David. He grew up in Nazareth as a devout Jew and was apprenticed to his father's trade. He drew no attention until in his early thirties he left his work, announced the coming of God's kingdom, gathered followers around him, spoke with exceptional fire and force and performed miracles of healing. After a mere three years his career finished brutally on a cross. Yet within a very short time his followers were everywhere saying he had risen from death, and broadcasting the coming of his kingdom. A century after Jesus' birth, the Christian faith had penetrated every level of society.

How does all this about Jesus link in with the Bible?

Jesus loved the Old Testament. For him the Old Testament was the holy word of God and the centre of his faith. He was brought up to love it and read it daily. But even here Jesus' remarkable authority can be seen. He did not simply accept it and submit to it like any other ordinary believer; he handled it as if he were its author and creator. 'You have heard that it was said . . . but I tell you . . .' is a familiar refrain in the Sermon on the Mount. This attitude to the law played no small part in his ultimate condemnation: according to the temple officials he had committed blasphemy by his arrogance, acting with an authority as if he were an equal to the sacred writings.

The first Christians used the Old Testament. After Jesus' resurrection the first Christians continued to worship with other Jews and during this period they tried to explain how the Old Testament writings pointed ahead to him. Most probably, relevant passages of the Old Testament were drawn together and began to be circulated as a separate document which the Christians used as a tool to convince fellow-Jews.

Stories about Jesus were collected. Alongside the use of the Old Testament as witness to the claims of Jesus, stories about him were written down and circulated. People were anxious to know about his teaching and his miracles. Eventually many of these accounts found their way into the Gospels which bear the names of Matthew, Mark, Luke and John, acquiring an authority equal to that of the Old Testament.

Apostles wrote letters, and a final development took place when these letters, from such Christian leaders as John, James, Peter and Paul, were accepted by the second generation of Christians as inspired by God. This was only to be expected. The churches needed authoritative guidance and it seemed quite natural to give to the apostles of Jesus an obedience they would have given him.

Thus by the end of the first century the shape of the New Testament was more or less what we have now. Although it was not until AD363 that the church gave final and official approval to a canon, to all intents and purposes the form was already fixed.

So within a few decades of the start of the Christian church an important position had been reached. Both Old and New Testaments were regarded as the word of God. This whole collection of books was **inspired** by God, **revealed** God's full salvation and was the church's **authority** for true Christian faith and practice.

THE INSPIRATION OF THE BIBLE

The word 'inspiration' means 'God-breathed'. It comes from the belief that every human being has his or her lungs inflated by God's breath at birth, and that at death one's breath was given back to him. Heroic figures like the prophets were thought to have been inspired with a fuller burst of divine breath than ordinary mortals. Logically then, the sacred writings must have received a special anointing, because they came from men specially inspired by the breath of God. So Paul reminds Timothy that the Old Testament was inspired by God and is 'useful for teaching the truth, rebuking error, correcting faults, and giving instruction for right living' (2 Timothy 3:16).

Inspiration was the means by which the Bible gained God's authority. But what is the meaning of the rather different idea of 'revelation'? Here we are thinking of *what* God communicates to us rather than simply how he did it. God in his revelation made certain things known to us through the inspired writers.

This distinction is crucial to get hold of. The Christian believes that everything in the Bible is inspired, but not everything has the same importance as revelation. Some parts of the Bible reveal God more fully and more clearly than others. Take two books, Leviticus and the Gospel of John. Both are inspired. But it is quite obvious that from the viewpoint of Christian truth John's Gospel is far more important as revelation than Leviticus. Yet both are crucial to the unfolding drama of salvation. The story grows from somewhat undeveloped ideas of God and his ways in the early parts of the Old Testament, on to the clearer teaching of the prophets and into the full light of the New Testament.

The point of **revelation** is that the Bible witnesses to God's salvation in Christ. The whole purpose of **inspiration** is that this process should be effective. The Holy Spirit inspired the writers of the different books, and he continues to use them as tools through which he makes Jesus Christ known and builds up the Christian family. The Bible is not the only tool by any means. God uses preaching, fellowship, the sacraments and other

131

means of grace to bring people to himself. But the Bible is the main artery of inspiration which links us today with God's word first spoken. We can be sure that his revelation in the Bible can be relied on because the Holy Spirit inspired the human writers to record a reliable account of what God did in history and what his will is.

As intelligent people we are bound sometimes to wonder, 'Are all the Bible's words inspired? Does its inspiration include issues such as human history and how the world began?' A full answer to these questions would take us beyond the scope of this book. But we need to keep the following guidelines in mind:

Remember what the Bible is about. It is not a comprehensive Encyclopedia of Life but a book about God and his great offer of salvation. It is such a remarkable book that we are tempted to use it to explain everything in life or even as a kind of 'railway timetable', but this is false to what it is. For example, the Bible is supremely indifferent to the question, 'How was the universe formed and made scientifically?' Its attention is on the fact that God created it for his glory.

Remember the divine and human elements in the Bible. They jostle side by side. The Holy Spirit used human beings, and he did not suppress their humanity as he did so. So not surprisingly we find evidence in their writings that these were men of their own times, and we shall need to take such cultural factors into account when we read the Bible. This does not in any way undermine their value for us, but reminds us again that the Bible is a historical book. The Holy Spirit of God used ordinary people in particular times and places to be channels of his marvellous revelation.

AUTHORITY

The authority of the Bible stems not from itself but from its author. It has authority because it is God-inspired. But what kind of authority does the Bible possess?

It helps to distinguish 'external' and 'internal' authority.

External authority is possessed by a person because a recognized group in society has given him or her power. So our friendly neighbour may don his uniform and become our friendly police officer. He now has an authority which is official and external.

Internal authority rests in the quality either of an impressive life or of acquired knowledge. For example, millions of Indians during Gandhi's lifetime regarded him as their guru and 'authority'. They paid attention to his words and example. But for most of his life he possessed no external authority at all. Within the Christian church we could say that the authority of a bishop is external whereas that of a saint is internal.

Transferring this distinction to the Bible, it is clear that the authority of the Bible is almost totally internal. Of course, the church regards the Bible as authoritative, yields to it and wants its members to believe it. But this cannot be imposed—it has to be accepted. The enquirer has to be convinced that this book is what Christians claim. If it does not bear the seal of God's signature there is no reason why you or I should accept it or give it our allegiance. Yet down the centuries millions of people who have read the Bible with an open mind, anxious to find the living God of whom it speaks, have found him. And this has led them to recognize that in this book lies the authority not of men but of God. The Bible has an authority which consists not in learned words but in transformed lives—a 'gospel-authority', which is 'God's power to save all who believe'.

27

The Authority of Jesus' Teaching

We have grown so used to thinking of Jesus as a great teacher that we forget how breathtaking that fact is. The teachings of a comparatively obscure man from Palestine nearly two thousand years ago are still the inspiration and guide of millions of Christians today. Why do they have such impact?

Our search for the answer must start with the actual teachings of Jesus in the Gospels, and two features are most impressive about them.

STRANGE AUTHORITY

Jesus taught with a strange authority. First-century teachers were, of course, plentiful. Many Rabbis went about proclaiming the law and interpreting its commandments. There were two main traditions of teaching: Shammai, a leading traditionalist, and Hillel, who was more modern and outward-looking. Followers of both schools were careful to pick their way through the minefield of interpretation by weighing the authority of bygone scholars: 'Rabbi Hillel said this but... on the other hand Rabbi Shammai taught that...' The greatest of authorities appealed to was, of course, Moses who received God's law in the first place. It was heretical to go beyond this fountain of truth—and whoever did was in trouble. But Jesus came with teaching that was startling in its simplicity and truth. 'You have heard that it was said (Moses said it) "Do not commit adultery". But I tell you that anyone who looks at a woman lustfully has already committed adultery with her in his heart.' Or, 'You have heard that it was said (again the hearers would have picked up the implied reference to Moses) "Do not break your oath . . ." But I tell you, do not swear at all.'

In summary we can say that the teaching of Jesus falls into three clear divisions:

The call to the kingdom. A great deal of the earlier teaching seems to concentrate on setting out what God's kingdom is like and how we enter it. We must become like little children and learn to trust God as Father.

The standards of the kingdom. He revealed the way of living required of those who had entered the kingdom, in both personal and social forms. In this way the law was interpreted in his day. For Jesus the ethic of love dominated law.

The coming of the kingdom. Here we find a tension between what has already come and what is yet to be. The kingdom has arrived because Jesus himself has come. All who follow him belong already to the kingdom. But this kingdom is only partially fulfilled now; it awaits its consummation when Jesus, the Son of man, comes again.

Jesus' teaching showed a quiet assurance. 'I tell you' speaks of a direct authority, rather than the derivative authority which the scribes and religious lawyers had. His hearers would have been in no doubt. This man was claiming an authority superior to that of Moses. Indeed, he was claiming to speak for God.

Together with this we must draw attention to what he said about his Father. He spoke of God as his 'Abba'. This was an extraordinary way of talking about God in his time because for Jesus' contemporaries God was a deity, wonderful and awesome and separated from the life of human beings. If it was characteristic for Jews of Jesus' time to think of God as 'Father in Heaven', still it can be said with confidence that no one before Jesus made it his practice to address God simply as 'Abba'. This term 'Abba' spoke of intimacy; our word 'daddy' comes closest to it. And it is obvious that the relationship with his Father was at the basis of his assurance, in his teaching and in his behaviour.

Although Jesus' miracles are part and parcel of the Christian story, they are really secondary to his teaching. Thus, when a paralyzed man was carried to Jesus by four of his friends, before talking at all about this man's health Jesus says to him: 'My son, your sins are forgiven.' Some of the Rabbis present at once noted the apparent heresy: 'Only God can forgive sins; who does this man think he is?' The miracle that follows serves to drive home the point that they were quite right in making this deduction, 'So that you may know that the Son of man has authority to forgive sins . . . I say to you, get up, pack up your bed and go home.'

GREAT ATTRACTIVENESS

Jesus taught also with a wonderful attractiveness. What an amazing teacher he must have been! Not for him the technique of spinning webs of theological intricacy, the tedious homilies which obscured truth from the ignorant and illiterate. It would seem that most of his teaching was spontaneous, arising from personal encounters with people, responding to their questions, challenges and needs. He was clearly master of the thought-provoking epigram or arresting picture story. When he said something like 'It is harder for a rich man to go into heaven than it is for a camel to go through the eye of a needle', we need to imagine him saying this with laughter, everyone joining in the joke of a camel with a hump going through a tiny needle. But the joke conveyed a profound truth that things in real life get in the way of what really matters.

Jesus taught in parables and picture stories, drawing on nature, human life and practical experience. No wonder people hung on every word, crowding the houses where he visited, the places where he taught, the roads he passed along. The technique of teaching through parables and picture language was not new; most good teachers employed this tool. But in Jesus' hands this became the major vehicle for communicating the message of the kingdom.

PICTURE STORIES

Why did he choose this indirect method of speaking in parables? Much ink has been spilt by scholars on this question. It may partly have been because it enables attention to be caught. There is nothing like a good story to arouse interest, and Jesus exploited the fun and the irony provided by parables. There is something extremely paradoxical about a good shepherd abandoning a whole flock because one sheep has got lost. Again, people do not normally sell up everything to buy one pearl; guests do not normally refuse an invitation to a good feast, especially in poverty-stricken Palestine; servants do not normally owe ten thousand talents; people who work for one hour do not usually get the same amount as those who work all day. And in Jesus' parable of the Good Samaritan, none of his hearers could have imagined that a Samaritan could possibly be the hero of a story. Picture a prejudiced Ulsterman telling a story in which the hero is a Catholic priest.

But there is probably another reason why Jesus spoke in parables. Central to most of the parables is a challenge to people to decide for or against him. The direct method—'I am the Son of God and you had better take it or leave it'—would have infuriated half the population and stopped them exploring the question of Jesus for themselves. Because the message of Jesus was primarily about the kingdom of God—how to enter it, its values and its relationship with himself—the method of the parable allowed people to make decisions, even to the point of becoming followers of the mysterious teacher from Nazareth, without tradition getting in the way.

Yet a point was reached where parables served less well. It is clear from the Gospels that at some stage in Jesus' ministry his teaching changed. At Caesarea Philippi, when Jesus was alone with his disciple he asked them: 'Who do people say that I am?' The disciples reported the common gossip about their Master: 'Some say you are one of the prophets; some people are also saying that you are Elijah returned to earth.' Then Jesus asked them the direct question, 'Who do you think I am?' And to this penetrating challenge Peter gave his historic answer: 'You are the Christ, the Son of the Living God.' This significant answer was the key that opened the disciples' understanding into the mystery of Jesus. From that point in the story of Jesus he turned away from parables and from talking to great crowds; from then on he spent time with the disciples teaching them about his destiny and preparing them for his death.

The time has come to return to the question with which we started this study. Why has this man of Nazareth had such impact on millions of people? The reason is not that he was such a splendid teacher—though he was; nor that he was such a fine man—which he also undoubtedly was. The reason lies in who he really was: in his identity with God the Father. We find him making assertions which do not come to us as exaggerated, unreal or absurd. They have about them the quiet certainty of divine authority. He declared that he was God's Son and God was his Father.

There are important passages where Jesus makes astounding claims which begin with the phrase 'I am'. This phrase has a backward glance to the Old Testament where God identified himself as 'I Am'. Throughout his ministry Jesus gave glimpses of his real nature which make the conclusion inescapable that he can only be understood by bringing in the idea of God. He forgave sins; he challenged the authority of the entire Jewish interpretation of the law, claiming to be superior to Moses; he went about healing people; he presented himself not first as a prophet but as the subject of all prophecy.

In studying Jesus as teacher, therefore, we are led beyond Jesus the man, to the Father he was so often talking about. Jesus demonstrated God; illustrated God. He gave God his right name 'Abba' and Christian experience subsequently discovers Jesus as the right place to meet God. Not simply as a doctrine to be discovered and learned, but as the very life and power of God himself. The challenge of Christianity is that we find God in Christ, not outside him.

28
How God Has Made Himself Known

Any important discovery about another person may be called 'revelation'. Think of human love or friendship and you will know that from intimacy springs revelation. It is the nature of love to reveal itself.

This is true of God's revelation except that, because he is the 'unknown' God, we cannot discover him at all without his help. Unless he reveals himself we cannot find him. This he does in four ways: through **creation**, through the **prophets**, through the whole **Bible** and, above all, through **Jesus Christ**. Putting it another way: through the seen Word, through the spoken Word, through the written Word and through the incarnate Word.

Revelation which comes to us through creation is often spoken of as 'general revelation'. This means that God has revealed himself in human history, through the beauty and order of creation, and in our own moral sense. This note is certainly there in the Bible. But we have to realize that such revelation is seriously affected by mankind's sin, so that instead of creation revealing God clearly, we have a distorted and incomplete vision of him.

Revelation through prophets, through the Bible and through Jesus Christ is called 'special revelation'. Because of our rebellion against him, God in his love and mercy has sent to us special messengers and prophets to call us back to him. The prophets through the Holy Spirit claimed to bring God's word to his people. Time and again they came crying, 'Thus says the Lord!' In time, the somewhat elusive words of the prophets gave way to the full and final revelation given in Jesus Christ— the incarnate Word, the Word made flesh. The letter to the Hebrews puts it this way: 'In the past God spoke to our forefathers through the prophets . . . but in these last days he has spoken to us by his Son.'

It is the testimony of the Bible and the Christian church that God has revealed himself perfectly and clearly through Jesus Christ. What is the essence of that revelation? That he is our Father and Deliverer and that his Son is the only way to him. The very heart of God's revelation, therefore, is the good news brought to us through Jesus Christ.

A very difficult problem relating to revelation is the place of the Bible. There are those scholars who argue that the Bible is not itself revelation but rather a record of God's revelation. It points to him. The moment we make the Bible to be itself revelation, they say, we end up worshipping a book instead of a living Lord. While we must acknowledge that this is a danger to be guarded against, it is extremely difficult to separate a record from the revelation it is witnessing to. How can we know the revelation except through its teaching and witness? The Bible is a faithful record and for that reason the Christian church from the very beginning has readily spoken of it as God's word, through which God's revelation in Christ has been conveyed to us. It is difficult to deny that in experience God's revelation comes to us through the very words of the Bible as it witnesses to Jesus Christ.

The Christian today has no need to be ashamed to confess that in Jesus Christ God has revealed himself finally, fully and perfectly. He is God's last and best Word, and we must carry this controversial message humbly to others, to share with them what we have learnt.

29

Does the Bible Speak Today?

Many millions of people in the world are convinced that the Bible speaks today—or, to be precise, that God speaks to them through it. The popularity of the Bible continues unabated, and it remains a world bestseller. The Bible, rather than forms of worship or doctrinal statements, holds Christians together, since all Christian churches and believers reckon it to be central to their faith. But this does not mean that all Christians are agreed about its interpretation or authority.

We may distinguish four approaches to the Bible, although of course, there are many who do not fit neatly into such categories:

'Fundamentalist' is a term used for those who have an uncritical approach to the Bible. A Fundamentalist will be likely to treat all parts of the Bible alike, giving a verse from Leviticus the same value as a verse from the Gospel of John. He or she will be suspicious of literary and historical study of the Bible, and will probably not use its findings. The Fundamentalist will be insistent on the 'infallibility' of the Bible, claiming that it is 'inerrant'.

Conservative Evangelicals work from the 'evangel' (gospel) at the heart of Scripture. The Bible is for them a collection of reliable, trustworthy books which testify to the crucified, risen Jesus. But conservative evangelical scholars will readily acknowledge the importance of historical research, use the tools of critical study, and be aware of the need to distinguish between the different types of literature in the Bible. Many will speak of the Bible's 'infallibility' and 'inerrancy' but may refer such terms to the Bible's infallible and sure testimony to Jesus Christ and his salvation. Other conservatives, however, prefer to speak of the 'trustworthiness' of the Bible, drawing attention to its complete reliability as a guide to belief and action.

Liberals may vary from a mild scepticism about the value of the Bible to a radical distrust. What is common to liberals is the view that historical criticism has made it impossible to treat the Bible as an infallible guide. Yet they are not keen to break the link between God and the Bible, and it is common for liberals to say that 'the Bible contains the word of God'. This has the advantage of dealing with different texts in different ways. But it has a crucial weakness. Who decides which parts of the Bible are the word of God and which are not?

Radicals see the Bible as a collection of ancient texts which cannot address us directly today. On this view, the culture of Bible times is so different from our own that it is impossible for the two to meet. The Bible may offer us suggestions about how the first Christians coped with problems of faith and conduct, say the radicals, but we ought to translate these into the 'myths' and culture of our own time, and not to regard the Bible itself as our 'normative' basis for faith and doctrine.

HISTORY AND FAITH

For the majority of Christians, the extreme positions do not offer viable bases for faith.

Fundamentalism is weakened by its simplistic disregard of the original intention of Scripture, and by its tendency to neglect nearly 200 years of historical research.

Biblical critics have certainly made some sweeping statements which have not stood up for long; their 'assured results' have not always proved very assured. But critical studies have been very valuable in many ways. They have often shown, for example, how the background of the times when particular Bible books were written affected the concerns of the writers, or how the Gospel writers used common material in a way that reflected what each of them saw as most important in Jesus' teaching. A blanket condemnation of all biblical criticism robs us of a lot of valuable insights. It can lead to a habit of trying to apply Bible teaching mindlessly, without asking the crucial questions along the way.

The other extreme, radicalism, is also unacceptable to many Christians. Radicals deny that critical study necessarily leads to scepticism about the origins of Christianity. Indeed, many will claim that, rather than making Jesus more difficult to find and understand, historical research has made the New Testament period more accessible and the mystery of Jesus in his living, dying and rising more gripping. The mistake of radicalism is to separate Bible times completely from our own, abandoning the attempt to find the links between the world of the Bible and modern Christianity.

INTERPRETING THE BIBLE

It is now widely realized, then, that someone today cannot simply lift a passage out of the Bible and just apply it to his or her situation as if it were written for that person alone. Certainly God does use the Bible in a direct, personal way. But a faithful interpretation requires us to be aware that Scripture had an original purpose, a primary reference to its own age. When we apply it to our own times, we must remember the differences and make any adjustments necessary. This does not in any way diminish the Bible's value and importance, but it does demand that we explore the background of the text and seek to discover what it originally meant.

For instance, we need to ask what sort of writing it is—is it poetry, full of images and word-pictures, or prose? It helps to know to whom the passage was addressed and what prompted its writing. We must learn to look back sympathetically to the original situation. We also need to develop the skill to distinguish between a timeless truth and its cultural expression.

All this means that today we are involved in a twofold interpretative task. We must both look back to the primary purpose of the writer and also try to relate this to our situation today. For example, the book of Hosea gives us beautiful and timeless truths about God's unquenchable love for his people. Yet the form of the writing will seem very strange to the modern mind. We owe it to Hosea to interpret his prophecy in our terms, so that the strength as well as the wonder of God's love is not lost.

THE BIBLE'S AUTHORITY

All Christian churches are agreed that the Bible is authoritative. By this we mean that it is our final court of appeal, the highest of all tests, to which all Christian theology and actions must bow.

While this is agreed, the Bible varies in its significance among Christian traditions. For many Protestant churches the Bible is claimed to be the sole authority. Anglicanism, however, differs slightly in that it attributes to the Bible a unique authority but also gives authoritative status to the four general councils and its own Thirty-Nine Articles of Religion. For Roman Catholics the Bible is placed in a partnership with tradition as two forms of God's revelation in Christ. But since the Second Vatican Council, Catholicism has given a clear 'normative' role to the Bible in the life of the church.

When we speak of the authority of the Bible, we are not talking about an intrinsic quality which belongs to a collection of old books because they are inspiring literature (although clearly they are that). We speak of an authority which belongs to God.

The authority of the Bible derives from the God who stands behind it and inspired its writers in a unique way. It also springs from the events which the Bible records. The Bible testifies to the deeds of God in history, of Jesus in his life and death, and of the Spirit in the church. As a reliable witness of these events, it conveys God's will for all who follow him. And so it is doing a great deal more than simply pointing back: it points to what God expects today from all who believe and obey, as well as indicating what is to come.

USING THE BIBLE TODAY

The Bible continues to flourish despite all attacks on it. It continues to feed the lives of millions of people, challenging unbelief, renewing faith and informing the life of the church. There has been little decline in its popularity or in its power to influence mankind. It is good to report that many churches place a great emphasis on Bible teaching, through house groups as well as through preaching. Organizations producing Bible-reading notes and group study aids influence the lives of millions through systematic Bible study. Through such aids, Christians are encouraged to include regular Bible reading in their discipline of prayer.

And yet in some ways Christian attitudes to the Bible have not changed for the better. It is now rare to find families reading the Bible together, and even among

Bible-loving Christians knowledge of the Scripture is not as deep or as extensive as it once was. This constitutes a challenge to the churches to stop the slide. Without building on the foundations, Christians' lives could easily become superficial and unduly influenced by the attitudes of modern society.

EPILOGUE

The Decade of Evangelism Begins

All the mainstream denominations have agreed to make the 1990s a 'decade of evangelism'. Yet many people find the very word 'evangelism' mysterious, and somewhat forbidding. It troubles some because it conjures up images of earnest missionaries preaching to innocent natives in former British Colonies. Others it appals, because they have seen American tele-evangelists threatening us with heavy black Bibles, when their own lives were corrupt.

No; evangelism does not have to be like that. So what is it?

Evangelism is 'sharing good news'. When you and I have good news of any kind we want to share it. Think of the time you passed that exam, had your baby, got that job, passed your driving test. You were bursting to tell someone; and you no doubt did.

In a similar way the first followers of Jesus Christ rushed out to tell a story—of God meeting them in a special way. Indeed, they used ideas quite similar to the good news mentioned above. They said that following Jesus was like the experience of 'new birth'; like finding your way home after a long journey; like making up after a fierce quarrel with someone you love dearly.

Not so long ago, at a party, I met a young man called Pat. Pat was one to speak his mind: 'You won't get me in church, Bishop, and do you know why? I'm not good enough. I like my pint, and my cigs and my flutter on the horses.

'Mind you,' he continued, 'I admire people like you. You really believe it, don't you. I'd like to have some purpose to my life.'

It so happened that I came from Pat's kind of background and the conversation that followed was friendly, though fairly frank. It went something like this:

Bishop George Pat, you said something like, 'I'm not good enough to be a Christian'. I fully agree with you. You're certainly not good enough. But then neither am I! I can tell you I'm far from perfect; just a normal struggling man.

Pat Well, how come you're a bishop then? I understand you come from Dagenham, my kind of background. Are you specially religious, to have got where you have?

Bishop Not particularly. I have to admit that I find the church's way of doing things difficult to take at times. I hate pomp and ceremony; I prefer simple things to ornate. But that isn't the essence of Christianity. Years ago I made an important discovery. I stumbled on the fact that God loves us—so much that he gave his Son for us. I remember the period in my life when it all came together, and I realized that Jesus is a real person, alive today. It sounds very dramatic, but it wasn't really. It was just a quiet realization that God exists, that he loves us all so much that he entered our world to find us—lost failures heading for death. And to rescue us.

That was something like what we said. Pat was interested, even impressed. I encouraged him to start reading the New Testament and even to give church a try one day. I wonder if he did?

But the conversation actually troubled me and still does.

It troubles me when I see ordinary people like Pat going through life without a mature faith to guide and help them. It troubles me when I see Christianity being confused with church. It troubles me when people see Jesus Christ as just a figure in history, remote from the lives of those he came to reach. It troubles me when people like Pat ask sincere questions, and the church does not appear to offer answers.

And it troubles me most of all because I *know* that the Christian faith is exciting and worthwhile, and yet so many people are going through life without its strength and richness.

So Christians have a tough job on their hands if they are to convince the Pats of this world that their faith is worth bothering about. How can it be done?

The first step is for Christians to start living the Christian faith. I know that many, many do. There are wonderful things done by the church and Christian people, and that cannot be denied. But nothing is so effective as the lives of committed and enthusiastic people. I don't mean people who come across as pious, with embarrassing religious language and so on. I mean people who are living the Christian faith, putting it into action. And who are not afraid of talking about it when the right moment comes. If we believe it, we should be showing it in our lives. There is a strong practical element in Christianity—it has to be lived where we live and where we work.

The second thing is that we should not be ashamed to talk about our faith, in all kinds of ways and situations. We have a clear message and it is understandable.

Christianity is essentially following Jesus Christ. Now all reasonable people are prepared to agree that he was an impressive man who has changed the world through his message. The sticking-point comes when Christians claim that God raised Jesus from the dead. That is an embarrassment to many people. We know that dead men don't rise again; and the resurrection seems like a cruel hoax. The evidence has to be studied in an open-minded way. I remain convinced that the only way to account for the rise of Christianity is on the basis that it is true—Jesus did rise from death.

But faith in Christ does not rest in vague hopes or intellectual arguments—that God exists, that Jesus rose. More persuasive still is the living experience of this faith. All Christians will want to say in their own words and their own way that God has revealed himself to them—through intellectual struggle, through doubt and fear, through challenge to the complacency of a busy but empty life, through the witness of another, through prayer, through the sacraments, through the lives of saints and others.

Like Geraldine, a twenty-eight-year old young lady I met fleetingly last year in St Peter's Hospice, Taunton. I had been called in by the Chaplain to confirm her. She was dying of cancer and there she lay, an emaciated figure but with the most glorious red hair.

I was told that Geraldine had come into the hospice some months before with hardly any real faith. But through the ministry of the doctors, nurses and chaplains she felt the closeness of God, and wanted to receive Communion before she died. It was a moving experience for me and a few others as she entered into the simple confirmation service, saying her parts with gasps but with full conviction: 'Do you turn to Christ? *I turn to Christ*. Do you repent of your sins? *I repent of my sins*. Do you renounce evil? *I renounce evil*.'

Within a few days Geraldine was dead, but her faith had carried her through her final months with great courage. There was no question to those who knew her of this being a mere deathbed repentance. Here was a turning to God which was real, sincere and life-changing.

But beyond what Christians can do, there is something that God can do for us. To those who are humble enough to seek the living God, that same God is humble enough to be found by us and to enter the restrictions of our human experience.

John's Gospel tells the story of a Jewish leader, Nicodemus, coming to Jesus by night and asking him questions. At one point in the conversation Jesus changes the subject and says:

'Nicodemus, unless a person is born again by water and the Spirit, he cannot see the kingdom of God.'

The rest of the account teases out what Jesus meant. The spiritual new birth takes place when men and women of good faith are prepared to follow Christ. Then God through his Spirit makes our lives his home, giving us meaning and purpose.

Perhaps I have made it seem all too simple. Well, it is simple—and yet mysterious at the same time. I am still discovering the wonder of God and his world every day I live. I thank God for the time I started my journey on the Christian way. And I thank God for his faithfulness to me on it.

So the Decade of Evangelism begins. Will the churches of Britain have more members by the year 2001? Will Britain be a more obviously Christian nation than in 1991? Or, to bring it closer to home, will there be more Christians in your locality?

I think it comes down to the health of the local churches. A healthy church—one that is healthy in worship, prayer and its contribution to the community in which it is set—cannot but grow. People are genuinely interested in Jesus, and when they see his way of living reflected in a local group of Christians, they will want to join them.

It is my expectation as Archbishop that the church I am associated with will be open, healthy and growing. Indeed, it is my hope that there will be some readers of this book who, up to now, have been on the fringe of church life but who will be encouraged to embark on the adventure of faith which is the essence of following Christ. Follow him—and you will not be disappointed.

JESUS: LIFE OR LEGEND?

Carsten Thiede

Can we know what Jesus was really like? How much of the traditional account is reliable, how much myth?

Nearly twenty centuries have passed since Jesus lived and died. And the story of his life and teaching exerts a powerful hold on the human imagination. Yet over the last few generations many writers have questioned the evidence about Jesus. He has been portrayed as a clown, an obsessive, a new-age guru . . .

Carsten Thiede looks at the languages, the contemporary sources, the unpublished finds, the Jewish and Roman setting of the time of Jesus. He considers the evidence of the New Testament Gospels, but also the references to Jesus in other writings, including the mysterious 'gnostic gospels'.

Carsten Thiede is an expert in the manuscripts, the archaeology and the history of the first century. He has lectured at the universities of Oxford, London and Geneva. He is a member of council of Germany's Institute for Education and Knowledge. His published work includes *The Earliest Gospel Fragment?* and *Simon Peter: from Galilee to Rome*.

ISBN 0 7459 1917 0

THE BIBLE: FACT OR FANTASY?

John Drane

Miracles, people rising from the dead, a man who claimed to be God—the Bible contains some sensational material. If these things really happened, they are vitally important for all time.

But is the Bible 'true'? Has its truth been disproved by discoveries in history, archaeology or science? Do the Bible's stories and its teaching still ring true today?

John Drane, Lecturer in Religious Studies at Stirling University, Scotland, has written popular introductions to the Old and New Testaments, and the best-selling Jesus and the Four Gospels. He has presented religious programmes on television. His doctoral research was on the Gnostics. In this book he brings his talents as a scholar and communicator to bear on the central question of the Bible's trustworthiness and relevance today.

ISBN 0 7459 1300 8

CHRISTIANITY ON TRIAL

Colin Chapman

This book sets out the case for and against Christian beliefs in a way that invites a verdict.

Colin Chapman has put together a collection of over 1,000 quotations, representing the greatest thought from the first century to the twentieth. They cover the deepest human questions. Christian claims are set out, tested and compared with alternatives from other major religions, thinkers and ideologies.

ISBN 0 7459 1273 7

WHOSE PROMISED LAND?

Colin Chapman

It is not easy to be dispassionate about this issue. Whose is the 'promised land', the land the Israelis call Israel, the Palestinians call Palestine? What arguments, claims and counter-claims lie behind the pioneer spirit of the settlers, the conflict, the violence, the refugee problem, the uprooting of families?

This book outlines the claims, then traces the story behind them, going right back to the time of the Bible, the basis for the Jews' claims to the land. What do the Bible's prophecies mean? How were the promises and prophecies made to ancient Israel understood by Jesus and the first Christian community? How should they be understood today? Is there a way forward?

Colin Chapman has been working with university students in different countries in the Middle East since 1968. He has had to face the issues first-hand. His aim in this book is to be fair in facing the issues and constructive in putting forward a way of peace.

ISBN 0 7459 1871 9

PILGRIMS' LONDON

Robert H. Baylis

Discover London's rich Christian heritage with the help
of this thoroughly practical book, packed full of
interesting sites to visit: historic churches, statues,
monuments, gravestones, portraits . . .

London has been home to many great Christian
personalities, and here some of the worldwide
confessions—Baptists, Methodists, Salvationists—were
born. The city is full of reminders of lives and events.
Piece the story together with the help of this book. Easy-
to-follow maps locate the sites. A-Z pen portraits
introduce the movements and personalities. Each
historical period has its own introduction. All sorts of
things are explained, from styles of church architecture to
when the museums are open.

0 7459 1645 7

A selection of top titles from LION PUBLISHING

JESUS: LIFE OR LEGEND? Carsten Thiede	£4.99 ☐
THE BIBLE: FACT OR FANTASY John Drane	£2.99 ☐
CHRISTIANITY ON TRIAL Colin Chapman	£5.95 ☐
WHOSE PROMISED LAND? Colin Chapman	£4.99 ☐
PILGRIMS' LONDON Robert H. Baylis	£4.99 ☐
SPIRITUAL AWAKENING Shirwood Eliot Wirt (ed.)	£4.95 ☐
SPIRITUAL POWER Shirwood Eliot Wirt (ed.)	£5.99 ☐
LISTENING TO YOUR FEELINGS Myra Chave-Jones	£3.99 ☐
TEENAGE BELIEFS David Day and Philip May	£4.99 ☐
FOR THE LOVE OF SANG Rachel Anderson	£3.99 ☐
LOVE NEVER ENDS Jenny Richards	£2.99 ☐
SHADOW OF WAR Gerda Erika Baker	£3.99 ☐

All Lion paperbacks are available from your local bookshop or newsagent, or can be ordered direct from the address below. Just tick the titles you want and fill in the form.

Name (Block letters) _____

Address _____

_____

_____

Write to Lion Publishing, Cash Sales Department, PO Box 11, Falmouth, Cornwall TR10 9EN, England.

Please enclose a cheque or postal order to the value of the cover price plus:

UK: 80p for the first book, 20p for each additional book ordered to a maximum charge of £2.00.

OVERSEAS INCLUDING EIRE: £1.50 for the first book, £1.00 for the second book and 30p for each additional book.

BFPO: 80p for the first book, 20p for each additional book.

Lion Publishing reserves the right to show on covers and charge new retail prices which may differ from those previously advertised in the text or elsewhere, and to increase postal rates in accordance with the Post Office.